ACTIVITIES FOR CHILDREN
IN THERAPY

About the Authors

Susan T. Dennison, A.C.S.W., L.C.S.W., has practiced as a clinical social worker for over twelve years in a variety of settings, providing counseling services to children. For over eight of those years she was a program administrator. Currently, Susan is on the faculty of Florida State University and has a consulting business. She has written two other books on kids' group therapy. Susan lives with her husband and son in Miami, Florida.

Connie K. Glassman, M.A., C.C.C., practiced as a speech and language pathologist in a rehabilitation setting for over ten years, five of which she was director of the department. She then studied art and worked in museum administration as the editor of the newsletter for the Bass Museum of Art in Miami Beach. Currently, she is a stuttering specialist in private practice and illustrates books with special education themes. Connie lives in Miami Beach, Florida with her husband and two children.

ACTIVITIES FOR CHILDREN IN THERAPY

A Guide for Planning and Facilitating Therapy
with Troubled Children

By

SUSAN T. DENNISON, M.S.W.

Consultant/Professor, Florida State University

and

CONNIE K. GLASSMAN, M.A.

Speech and Language Pathologist

CHARLES C THOMAS • PUBLISHER
Springfield • Illinois • U.S.A.

Published and Distributed Throughout the World by

CHARLES C THOMAS • PUBLISHER

2600 South First Street

Springfield, Illinois 62794-9265

© *1987 by* CHARLES C THOMAS • PUBLISHER

ISBN 0-398-05294-8

Library of Congress Catalog Card Number: 86-23007

With THOMAS BOOKS *careful attention is given to all details of manufacturing and design. It is the Publisher's desire to present books that are satisfactory as to their physical qualities and artistic possibilities and appropriate for their particular use.* THOMAS BOOKS *will be true to those laws of quality that assure a good name and good will.*

Printed in the United States of America
Q-R-10

Library of Congress Cataloging in Publication Data

Dennison, Susan T.
  Activities for children in therapy.

  Bibliography: p.
  1. Play therapy. 2. Psychotherapists and patient.
I. Glassman, Connie K. II. Title. [DNLM: 1. Psy-
chotherapy--in infancy & childhood. 2. Psychother-
apy--methods. WS 350.2 D411a]
RJ505.P6D46 1986   618.92'89'1653   86-23007
ISBN 0-398-05294-8

FOREWORD

THE Dennison Individual Therapy Practice model guides the practicing clinician through the maze of clinical/theoretical issues and questions. It helps the therapist conceptualize the child's problem, what behaviors need to be learned/changed, and what therapeutic activities can be engaged in with the child to bring about the therapeutic goals. The model is also useful because it outlines practical and objective methods of assessing whether therapeutic goals have been attained.

The authors have provided an invaluable service, particularly to beginning therapists who frequently have difficulty making the transition from textbook theory to clinical practice, from academic knowledge to a full understanding of what actually happens in therapy, how it happens, how to know when change has occurred, and, most important of all, how to control the course of therapy to bring about the desired outcome.

The present text takes much of the hard work out of planning and implementing therapy with children. Mrs. Dennison and Mrs. Glassman take the practitioner step-by-step through each decision point in the therapy process, demonstrating clearly how questions, issues and answers change at each stage, from the initial establishment of the therapeutic relationship through termination. The authors concern themselves equally with activities aimed at strengthening the bond between therapist and child and facilitating the *process* of therapy, and with what actually goes on at each stage—the content of therapy. The section which deals with actual exercises and activities designed to bring about therapeutic goals will bring smiles to the faces of therapists who are faced week after week with planning activities which are enjoyable and engaging to the child, as well as accomplishing what the Dennison model terms process and content goals.

Mrs. Dennison and Mrs. Glassman are to be congratulated for bringing their years of experience with children to the pages of this book in an organized, well-conceptualized and useful format, which both beginning and more seasoned therapists will use as a how-to-do-it guide in their therapy with children.

DIANE V. LILLESAND, Ph.D.
Clinical Psychologist

INTRODUCTION

Purpose of the Book

THE VERBAL APPROACH to child therapy by itself is typically ineffective, particularly with the more disturbed youngster. Many sensitive and difficult issues can be surfaced through non-threatening play activities as an alternative. Professionals can then use their expertise for processing issues with the child rather than for eliciting the disclosure. *Activities for Children in Therapy* provides the mental health professional with a wide variety of therapeutic activities to be used with the five-to twelve-year-old troubled child. These activities have been designed as enjoyable games that both the therapist and child can play in the context of therapy.

Although there are a number of books on the market regarding individual therapy with children, few provide the clinician with planning suggestions. This text was developed to address the void in the literature. Many experienced professionals today are tired of hearing more about theories. Instead, they want some concrete ideas for interventions that will be effective in counseling the child of elementary school age. This book has been designed specifically with those practice-based issues in mind. Child therapists will find that this is a resource manual that will meet the needs they face in their work on a daily basis.

Activities for Children in Therapy has been written primarily for professionals who provide counseling to children. However, the material can be adapted for use by speech/language pathologists, art therapists, and other related professionals. This book can also be used to train the beginning therapist.

Children with emotional problems are the targeted population to benefit from the activities in this book. This population, of course, covers a wide variety of youngsters. For example, these children could have any of the following difficulties that are secondary to the emotional factor: physical handicaps, neurological impairments, learning disabilities, hyperactivity, mental retardation, or multi-problems.

The activities are intended to be used in individual therapy, but with some modification they can be used in a group setting. For example, the counselor could incorporate the material into a group therapy program, or a special education teacher could use them in the classroom. Clinicians providing these allied services will need to evaluate the appropriateness and applicability of these activities for the child's treatment.

Secondary purposes of this book include providing "An individual Therapy Practice Model" (Chapter One), "An Assessment Guide for Individual Therapy" (Chapter Two) and supplementary references (Appendices A, B, C, and D). The contents of Chapters One and Two provide a simple and straightforward framework for the use of the activities in the following six chapters. Also, these initial chapters provide the clinician with a new viewpoint of individual therapy, along with some practical planning suggestions. Additional references on child development, individual therapy with children, and clinical assessment are listed in Appendix A. A carefully chosen list of evaluative scales and checklists for the individual assessment of children is given in Appendix B. Appendices C and D provide additional games, along with children's books and magazines, to supplement the activities of this text. Appendix E contains a sample report for assessing a child for individual therapy. Finally, the answers to response specific activities in Chapters Three through Eight are listed in Appendix F.

Content Areas of Activities

The heart of the book consists of activities in the following six content areas:

1. Chapter Three: "Activities Related to Relationship Building and Self-Disclosure"
2. Chapter Four: "Activities Related to Affective Awareness and Communication"
3. Chapter Five: "Activities Related to Family"
4. Chapter Six: "Activities Related to Social Skills"
5. Chapter Seven: "Activities Related to School"
6. Chapter Eight: "Activities Related to Termination and Follow-up"

The sequencing of these six chapters has been purposeful. A program of therapy begins with relationship-building activities (Chapter Three) in order that a trusting therapist/child relationship is assured. Once established, the therapist can determine the more specific areas (Chapters Four through Seven) to be addressed with a particular child. Thus, clinicians may use selectively the activities in Chapters Four through Seven, choosing those that are relevant to the child's treatment needs. Chapter Two contains specific guidelines for determining areas of therapeutic intervention.

Termination is the last step of therapy, and activities from Chapter Eight are used to elicit grieving regarding the end of treatment and to acknowledge therapeutic progress. It is essential that a therapist allow time for this termination experience. Troubled children often have many unhealthy endings in their lives and need to have a corrective experience with the therapist. In some cases, professionals may also decide to schedule follow-up sessions with a youngster as a way of maintaining therapeutic gains. Activities have also been provided in Chapter Eight for follow-up sessions.

Format of the Activities

All the activities in Chapters Three through Eight are designed in the following format:

(1) A high and low age level version of each activity is provided. The lower age group activity is intended for ages five through eight and appears on the front of each page. The higher age group activity is for the nine-through twelve-year-old and appears on the back of each page. Because most problem children function below their grade level, the activities have been developed for children functioning beneath the average youngster in their age group. Therefore, professionals should increase the skill level of the activities for the brighter child. Readers may still find that this age guide is not consistent with all children, depending on their skill level and areas of interest. Accordingly, professionals should choose activities or modify them based on the individual needs and response of each child.

(2) Each activity is based on a theme for the chapter content area (i.e., theme of learning about the types of feelings one can have from Chapter Four on "Activities Related to Affective Awareness and Communication"). These themes are listed at the beginning of each chapter. The themes have been sequenced in a logical order and in such a way as to assure variety in the activities. Readers should feel free to individually sequence the themes and activities based on the needs of each child and therapist.

(3) Instructions have been provided at the top of each activity sheet. These directions are simple and straightforward. They are easily identified by locating on the activity sheet the drawing tools required (pencil, crayon, etc.).

(4) The answers to wordfinds, crossword puzzles, and other response specific activities can be found in Appendix F.

(5) At the bottom of some activity pages, a "thinker box" has been provided. The questions or statements in these boxes are intended to elicit further disclosure from the child on the theme of the page. Readers can optionally use this material in their sessions.

(6) The length of time for each activity will vary. For example, a therapist may find that what lasts a half hour for one child may only last five minutes for another. In the latter case, the therapist will have to decide if a theme more relevant to the child needs to be addressed or if another activity from that same chapter would be more effective. Readers are encouraged to use more than one activity in a session, depending on the response of the youngster. At the same time, completion of as many activity sheets as possible in a session should not become the objective. Rather, the probing and discussing of a particular issue are the ultimate goals. The activities only serve as non-threatening ways of eliciting disclosure.

Cautionary Notes

The reader will find that the activities in this book look similar to children's game books available for purchase by the general public. This similarity in presentation is intended to interest and motivate the child. The book is designed for use by professionals only. Parents and other non-professionals should not use this material as a way of working with their own children. Information elicited through the activities is often of a sensitive nature. An inability to process or handle emotionally charged issues could be harmful to a child.

Professionals may want to share information generated through the activities with parents or significant others during appropriate times in the therapy process. This disclosure can be beneficial as long as the therapist is careful to interpret the findings for the parent and deal with the reactions. The confidentiality of the child must be kept in mind. A child's permission should be first obtained. The youngster should then be assured that only certain activity sheets will be shared. Some children may not be comfortable with any disclosure. Therapists will need to respect their wishes so as to assure the maintenance of a trusting relationship. An exception to this would be a therapist's responsibility to inform parents of a safety issue such as a child's plan to commit suicide or harm another.

Summary

Activities for Children in Therapy is a workbook for the professional in search of a motivating framework for therapeutic interventions with troubled children of elementary school age. The activities are designed to build a significant child/therapist relationship, surface problem areas, aid in resolving those problems and provide a healthy closure to the therapy relationship. Guidelines for the use, timing and rationale of the activities are provided through an Individual Therapy Practice Model (Chapter One) and an Assessment Guide (Chapter Two). Supplemental references are provided in Appendices, A, B, C, and D.

This is a "how-to-do-it" book for the mental health professional who is in need of new and creative interventions with children. It is intended that readers will individualize the material for each youngster. Also, it is hoped this book will serve as a stimulus for professionals to develop other avenues for working effectively with children.

ACKNOWLEDGMENTS

MANY PEOPLE have been instrumental in contributing to the completion of this work. Special thanks go to Elane Nuehring for her salient editorial feedback and Joyce Wirch for outstanding preparation of the final manuscript.

A personal thanks goes to our husbands, Joe Dennison and Stuart Glassman, who were forever patient and helpful during this project. And, finally, special appreciation goes to our children, Matthew, Jordan, and Ariel, who were always there as an inspiration.

S.T.D.

C.K.G.

CONTENTS

ACTIVITIES FOR CHILDREN
IN THERAPY

CHAPTER ONE

AN INDIVIDUAL THERAPY PRACTICE MODEL

THE Dennison Individual Therapy Practice Model is introduced and described in the present chapter. This model serves two major purposes for the reader. First, it provides a goal-focused approach to individual therapy with children. Second, it is a planning guide for the activities in Chapters Three through Eight.

Originally, this model was developed for K.I.D.S. Group Therapy[1] but now has been adapted for individual treatment. This approach combines several theoretical perspectives but is based primarily on a behavioral methodology. The model attempts to define therapy goals in such specific behavioral terms that the focus of treatment is clear throughout the counseling experience. As a result, therapists who follow the model will find that planning and facilitating sessions is easier and more effective.

The four major components of the Dennison Individual Therapy Practice Model are outlined in Table I. First, therapy is divided into three phases: initial, middle, and termination. Second, two types of goals (process and content) have been defined for each of those phases. Third, a primary and secondary goal emphasis guide has been provided to identify for the therapist which goals (process or content) are most important in each phase of therapy. Fourth, an activity guide has been presented in which the activity chapters of this book have been correlated with the three phases of the model.

Phasing of Treatment

Although this model's phasing of treatment into three time periods is not a new concept, it is an important one. Clinicians need to remember

---

[1]The K.I.D.S. program is a structured approach to group therapy with elementary age children. One of its major premises is the value of planned therapeutic play activities. At the same time, treatment is individualized through the modification of the program's components.

Dennison, Susan T.: A Handbook for K.I.D.S. Group Therapy. Miami, self-published 1980.

TABLE I

DENNISON INDIVIDUAL THERAPY PRACTICE MODEL/ACTIVITY GUIDE

INITIAL PHASE	MIDDLE PHASE	TERMINATION PHASE
Process Goals*	**Process Goals**	**Process Goals***
Primary Emphasis	Secondary Emphasis	Primary Emphasis
1. To initiate the child's attraction to the therapy setting.	1. To increase the child's attraction to the therapy setting.	1. To increase the child's attraction to other supports.
2. To initiate child's disclosure in sessions.	2. To increase the child's level of disclosure.	2. To have child acknowledge progress in therapy.
3. To initiate feelings of trust toward the therapist.	3. To increase feelings of trust with the therapist.	3. To have child grieve the ending of therapy.
Content Goals	**Content Goals***	**Content Goals**
Secondary Emphasis	Primary Emphasis	Secondary Emphasis
1. To assess the child's appropriateness for individual therapy.	These are the treatment goals determined individually for each child.	These are the same ones established in the middle phase of treatment.
2. To begin establishing treatment goals.		
Activities to Attain Goals	**Activities to Attain Goals**	**Activities to Attain Goals**
Chapter Three—"Relationship Building/Self-Disclosure."	Chapter Four—"Affective Awareness and Communication"	Chapter Eight—"Termination and Follow-up"
	Chapter Five—"Social Skills"	
	Chapter Six—"Activities Related to Family"	
	Chapter Seven—"Activities Related to School"	

* This indicates the goals that are of primary emphasis in each of the phases of treatment.

that the focus of therapy changes throughout treatment. For example, in the initial phase (see Table I), a relationship is established, assessment occurs and treatment goals are determined. By the middle phase, the therapist is able to address the problems precipitating the child's referral. Then, in the termination phase, therapy comes to a close. The youngster has an opportunity to grieve the ending of therapy, acknowledge progress made during treatment, and explore other sources of support. Understanding the trust of therapy in each of these phases has significant impact on a clinician's effectiveness.

Process and Content Goals

Addressing two sets of parallel goals simultaneously in treatment is one of the unique features of the Dennison model. This breakdown of goals has been done to clarify the dual focus of therapy throughout the treatment experience. When providing therapy to children, clinicians know they must not only deal with the presenting problems (i.e., content goals) but also those variables that motivate the child to come to sessions, disclose information, and trust the therapist (i.e., process goals).

In Table I, the reader will note that there are three different process goals for each phase. These goals are directed at creating an optimal setting and enhancing the therapist/child relationship so that disclosure, change and termination flow easily. The process goals remain constant for all clients. The means for attaining them may vary because every child responds to different interventions. However, their purpose, which is to ensure attention to the essential aspects of therapy, necessitate their presence for all clients.

The content goals, on the other hand, focus on the issues and problems that resulted in a child's referral for treatment. They are established in the initial phase after a period of assessment (see Table I). These goals are different for every child, since they reflect his/her particular problem areas. Content goals should be specific and measurable with examples of expected behavioral changes. It is also important to establish these goals so that they can be attained in a period of about three months of therapy. Clients and therapists alike need to experience a sense of accomplishment on a regular basis during the treatment process.

Primary and Secondary Goal Emphasis

The concept of primary and secondary goal emphasis, as seen in Table I, provides the reader a specific goal focus for each of the three phases. This distinction has been made because the two sets of goals are being addressed simultaneously throughout treatment. The therapist will need to know which goals (process or content) are of primary emphasis in each phase.

5

In the initial phase, the process goals are of primary emphasis, since the child has to be motivated to attend, disclose and trust in the sessions. During the middle phase, the primary emphasis switches to the content goals. It is during this period that the clinician can concentrate on the child's problem areas. After successful completion of the middle phase of therapy, the therapist and the child move into the termination phase. The process goals once again become primary with much attention being directed at successful closure.

Primary and secondary goal emphasis affects both planning and facilitating of therapy. An understanding of the goal focus in each phase will impact significantly on a clinician's effectiveness.

Activity Guide

The last major aspect of the Dennison model is the activity guide. In Table I, the reader will see that Chapters Three through Eight have been correlated with each of the three phases and appear at the bottom of each column. This coordination of the activity chapters with the model provides the rationale behind the selection and timing of the activities in this text. Readers will find that by understanding the Dennison model and following the activity guide, they should be able to more easily plan effective therapy sessions. Clinicians are also urged to use these guides when originating and timing any new interventions.

Treatment Implications of the Dennison Model

The Dennison model has been designed with goal attainment in mind. In addition to the activities provided in this text, other treatment implications of this model have been provided in Tables II (Attainment of the Initial Phase Goals), III (Attainment of the Middle Phase Goals) and IV (Attainment of the Termination Phase Goals). These tables delineate ways to attain the process and content goals that are specific to the needs of elementary age children. Therapists should refer to the appropriate table when they are conducting therapy in each phase. The guidelines in Tables II, III and IV need to be used with Table I to maximize the impact of therapy. The suggested means of goal attainment in Tables II, III and IV are not exhaustive. In fact, clinicians can use them as a guide to develop other ways to attain the process and content goals for each phase.

Initial, Middle and Termination Phases of Treatment

In the initial phase (Table II), a positive cue for therapy must be established. Hence, the process goals are of primary emphasis at this time. Therapists have to be most concerned about creating an attractive set-

TABLE II

ATTAINMENT OF INITIAL PHASE GOALS

PRIMARY EMPHASIS		SECONDARY EMPHASIS	
PROCESS GOALS	SUGGESTED MEANS OF ATTAINMENT	CONTENT GOALS	SUGGESTED MEANS OF ATTAINMENT
1. To initiate child's attraction to the therapy session.	a. Schedule sessions' length and frequency at child's level of functioning.	1. To assess the child's appropriateness for individual therapy.	a. Administer objective evaluative scales to child.
	b. Setting should be free of visual and auditory distractions.		b. Plan and evaluate child in assessment activities.
	c. Establish a session format for child's comfort and attention span.		c. Obtain feedback on child's problems from significant others.
	d. Plan a lot of variety in the activities.		d. Review history of child relevant to therapy assessment.
	e. Most activities should be based on a play not verbal approach to therapy.		e. Note observations of child behaviorally and affectively in sessions.
	f. Plan sessions so little disciplining is required.		
	g. Make sure the therapist and child are having fun together.		
	h. Instructions and lectures should be clear and brief.		
	i. Activities should be of interest to the child.		
	j. Process with child only what they liked about the sessions. Sessions should end on a positive note.		

7

TABLE II *(continued)*

ATTAINMENT OF INITIAL PHASE GOALS

PRIMARY EMPHASIS		SECONDARY EMPHASIS	
PROCESS GOALS	SUGGESTED MEANS OF ATTAINMENT	CONTENT GOALS	SUGGESTED MEANS OF ATTAINMENT
2. To initiate child's disclosure in session.	a. Therapist models disclosure as a stimulus for child to verbalize. b. Child should be regularly assured of the confidentiality of sessions. Disclosures to significant others regarding safety issues should be discussed with the child ahead of time. c. Child should always be aware of therapist's contact with significant others once therapy has begun. d. Plan non-threatening ways to elicit disclosure. e. Therapist should be realistic about child's expected level of disclosure. f. Child should be asked why they think they were referred for treatment. g. Therapist should inform child that therapy may end with assessment period. h. Process sessions with child each time. i. Therapist should ask child for activity suggestions.	2. To begin establishing treatment goals.	a. Therapist should analyze results from evaluative scales. b. Assessment data from observations of child in session should be compiled. c. Significant others' feedback should be reviewed. d. Realistic, short term behavioral treatment goals should be determined. e. A comprehensive assessment report should be written.

TABLE II *(continued)*

ATTAINMENT OF INITIAL PHASE GOALS

PRIMARY EMPHASIS		SECONDARY EMPHASIS	
PROCESS GOALS	SUGGESTED MEANS OF ATTAINMENT	CONTENT GOALS	SUGGESTED MEANS OF ATTAINMENT
3. To initiate feelings of trust toward the therapist.	a. Therapist should always be warm, honest and sincere with the child. b. Therapist should share some personal things about himself/herself to model for the child. c. A wide variety of experiences should be planned and shared between therapist and child. d. Sessions should be made comfortable and non-threatening. e. Positive processing should be done at the end of all sessions. f. Therapist can give treats to child to convey feelings of caring. g. Child should be asked to disclose at his/her comfort level. h. Child should be reminded of the confidentiality of session. i. Consistent contact should be promised and maintained with child whenever possible.		

TABLE III
ATTAINMENT OF MIDDLE PHASE GOALS

PRIMARY EMPHASIS		SECONDARY EMPHASIS	
PROCESS GOALS	SUGGESTED MEANS OF ATTAINMENT	CONTENT GOALS	SUGGESTED MEANS OF ATTAINMENT
1. To increase child's attraction to therapy setting.	a. Session length and frequency may need to be increased. b. Some changes may now be made with the session format and setting. c. Activities should be planned that have more challenge and surface some of the child's problem areas. d. Discussion time should now be increased and encouraged. e. Therapist should ask child for more input in the shaping of sessions. f. Processing at the end of sessions should now include the child's likes and dislikes.	These goals are individually determined for each child.	The means for attaining these goals are individually determined. The activities in Chapters Three through Eight and Appendices C and D would be some possible means used.
2. To increase the child's level of disclosure.	a. Therapist should model more intimate disclosure. b. Activities should address the content goals. c. Therapist may want to ask child how therapy is benefitting him/her. d. Child needs to be encouraged to deal with all feelings toward the therapist. e. Child should be asked to disclose and discuss problems he/she is experiencing.		

TABLE III *(continued)*

ATTAINMENT OF MIDDLE PHASE GOALS

PRIMARY EMPHASIS		SECONDARY EMPHASIS	
PROCESS GOALS	SUGGESTED MEANS OF ATTAINMENT	CONTENT GOALS	SUGGESTED MEANS OF ATTAINMENT
3. To increase feelings of trust with the therapist.	a. Therapist should regularly acknowledge special feelings toward the child.		
	b. Occasional treats and surprises can be given to the child to convey the significance of the relationship.		
	c. Child can be asked what the therapist means to him/her.		
	d. Child can be requested to do assignments outside sessions.		
	e. Discussion on child's life outside session should be increased.		
	f. Therapist can confront child on areas of resistance.		

TABLE IV
ATTAINMENT OF TERMINATION PHASE GOALS

PRIMARY EMPHASIS		SECONDARY EMPHASIS	
PROCESS GOALS	SUGGESTED MEANS OF ATTAINMENT	CONTENT GOALS	SUGGESTED MEANS OF ATTAINMENT
1. To increase child's attraction to other supports.	a. Plan sessions such that child explores with therapist other sources of support. b. Therapist has other supportive people in child's life attend some sessions. c. Child given assignments to elicit and learn how to use other supports. d. Skills of child further developed to more appropriately rely on other sources of support. e. Child can be asked to process what type of support will meet their needs.	These are the same as those developed for each child in the middle phase.	These are individualized based on the content goals.
2. To have child acknowledge progress made in therapy.	a. Therapist acknowledges his/her perception of child's changes. b. Activities and discussions should be planned on theme of therapy progress. c. In vivo experiences provided so child believes the progress made can now be maintained without therapy. d. No further disclosure on new problem areas should be allowed. e. Processing can include how child sees self differently in the current sessions as opposed to the initial ones.		

TABLE IV *(continued)*

ATTAINMENT OF TERMINATION PHASE GOALS

PRIMARY EMPHASIS		SECONDARY EMPHASIS	
PROCESS GOALS	SUGGESTED MEANS OF ATTAINMENT	CONTENT GOALS	SUGGESTED MEANS OF ATTAINMENT
1. To have child grieve the ending of therapy.	a. The frequency of sessions can be reduced. b. Therapist can share the significance of the relationship to himself/herself. c. Sessions planned to discuss the ending of therapy. d. Time should be allowed for child to grieve other unfinished endings. e. Awards or gifts given to child to acknowledge importance of the relationship. f. Reminders given regularly as to how many sessions remain. g. A celebration can be planned during the last sessions to signify the end and also to underscore the sense of accomplishment.		

ting, encouraging disclosure and building a trusting relationship. Assessment and the establishment of treatment goals (i.e., content goals) are part of this phase but must be secondary in importance.

Readers need to remember that the degree to which the process goals are attained in this phase will greatly determine the extent to which the treatment goals can be addressed in the middle phase. Therefore, the guidelines provided in Table II should be followed very closely, since goal attainment in the initial phase will greatly determine a child's response later in treatment.

By the middle phase (Table III), clinicians should find that their relationship with the child is well-established, disclosure occurs comfortably, and a level of trust has developed. Now, the issues and problems that resulted in a child's referral for therapy (i.e., content goals) can be given primary emphasis. As seen in Table III, the means to attaining these content goals will have to be individually determined for each child. Hopefully, by this point in therapy, clinicians will know the most effective ways to work with a particular youngster. Now, the task will be to work on the content goals with those interventions.

The last phase of therapy is termination (Table IV) and it is a crucial one. Primary emphasis is on the process goals in this phase. Enough time must be spent on the closure of the therapeutic relationship to ensure that the child has sufficient opportunity to resolve feelings toward the therapist. A healthy closure often provides a corrective experience for other unresolved endings in the child's life. For this reason, therapists must be careful that the sessions address therapy gains rather than new issues or problems. Children need to grieve the ending of treatment, acknowledge their progress and explore other sources of support (i.e., process goals). Readers should, as a result, follow closely the guidelines provided in Table IV for attaining these process goals.

Summary

The Dennison Individual Therapy Practice Model is outlined in this chapter. It provides the clinician with a framework for conducting individual therapy with children. Also, the model serves as a planning guide for the activities in Chapters Three through Eight.

Therapy via this model is divided into three phases: initial, middle and termination. Two types of goals (process and content) are defined for each phase. This dual-goal approach to therapy is one of the unique aspects of the Dennison model. Through this specification of two sets of goals, the reader is given a clearer understanding of the thrust of treatment in each phase.

Finally, other treatment implications of the model are provided for the three phases. With these guidelines and the activities in this book, the therapist has a wide variety of ideas for both planning and facilitating therapy sessions with children.

CHAPTER TWO

AN ASSESSMENT GUIDE FOR INDIVIDUAL THERAPY

AN ASSESSMENT procedure for individual therapy with children is provided in this chapter. This evaluative process is different from those diagnostic assessments used as a basis for referral such as the psychosocial, the intake, the DSM III workup and the psychological. One or several of these diagnostic evaluations may be available to the therapist as part of the child's record at the time of the referral. These procedures are usually intended to establish a diagnosis on a child and often are accompanied with some general treatment recommendations.

Once a child begins individual treatment, it is essential that another type of assessment is completed. This procedure has three purposes. The first purpose is the establishment of the client's readiness or appropriateness for individual therapy. The second purpose is the identification of problems that can be focused on in this treatment modality. Finally, a baseline of functioning in all treatment areas will be done through this evaluative procedure. The attainment of these three goals in this assessment will assure not only that the treatment modality utilized is appropriate but also that there is a basis for accountability.

In order to accomplish this comprehensive evaluation, an outline for an assessment report is suggested along with a logging method to organize and compile significant findings. An extensive list of assessment scales (Appendix B) and activities (Chapter Three) are also provided to accomplish such an assessment. This procedure is intended as a guide that clinicians can modify to meet the needs of a particular setting or client population.

Value of a Formal Assessment Procedure

When children are referred for therapy, it is essential to conduct a formal assessment. Unfortunately, after the usual diagnostics (i.e, intakes, psychosocials, etc.), many clinicians do not formally assess children before starting therapy. Even though a child may have had previous evaluations, these assessments will not have addressed the youngster's response to therapy with the current clinician. A formal assessment procedure may seem to be very time-consuming to the therapist. However, in the long run it saves time by assuring that the therapy is appropriate and individualized for maximum impact. The major benefits of a formal assessment are as follows:

(1) The appropriateness of individual therapy for the child is identified early in treatment.

(2) Children who would not benefit from individual therapy can be referred to a more appropriate treatment modality.

(3) Initial therapy sessions involve specific assessment tasks and thus are more predictable and comfortable for the child. Youngsters of elementary school age are more comfortable and less threatened when they come into structured sessions that follow a routine.

(4) The child is told at the beginning that treatment will be dependent on the outcome of the assessment. With this awareness, he/she will not be overly disappointed or hurt if treatment is terminated without a full course of therapy.

(5) The clinician's recommendations have more impact on parents and other involved professionals. A formal assessment is outlined with significant results that provide the rationale for a recommended treatment plan. A message of mutual respect is conveyed by the therapist to parents and professionals. The explanation of the evaluation and the findings assist those individuals in understanding the recommendations.

(6) The therapist is more confident of his/her role with a child after an assessment. This increased confidence is based on a better understanding of the child's problems and of the interventions that are effective in treating those difficulties.

(7) Treatment goals are measurable and behaviorally specific as a result of assessment. A child's current level of functioning in problem areas is determined and realistic goals are established. Also, the therapist's increased knowledge of the youngster will result in treatment expectations that are individualized and can be measured as therapy progresses.

(8) Expectations of treatment are established early. Parents and other involved professionals will have a better understanding of what therapy can accomplish for a particular youngster.

(9) The therapist is more accountable to the child, the parents and other involved professionals.

Readers can see that there are a number of important benefits to conducting a formal assessment. The advantages of this procedure directly impact on treatment conducted afterwards.

Guidelines for Setting Up Assessment Sessions

The developmental needs of children are different from those of both adult and adolescent clients. Therefore, the planning and facilitating of sessions will have to address those unique needs. Therapists may want to refer to material on child development in Appendix A for more specific information on this topic. The following guidelines for the assessment and subsequent therapy sessions with children take into account those developmental needs:

(1) The shorter attention span and memory skills of children necessitate that sessions be scheduled at least twice a week for thirty minutes to an hour. The attention span of the individual child will determine the exact length of time for therapy sessions.

(2) Young children require a therapy room that is free of outside auditory and visual distractions. Otherwise, it is difficult to keep them on task. The room should be free of any distracting materials that are within reach or sight. The ideal environment is a small room with a table, chairs and space on the floor to play.

(3) Children need to be assured of the confidentiality of sessions. Counselors should explain that there may be times when some information will have to be shared with parents. However, youngsters need to be assured that they will be told of that disclosure ahead of time.

(4) It is helpful to ask children why they feel they were referred for therapy. Many diagnostic impressions can be obtained by hearing their perceptions of why they need help.

(5) Children enjoy following a routine while at the same time having a variety of activities within that routine. For this reason, it is helpful to establish a format for sessions. This variety of tasks addresses the short attention span of youngsters between five and twelve years of age. The following is an example of a format for assessment and therapy sessions:

First Task:

A disclosure question is planned for each session and is answered by both therapist and child. As therapy progresses, these questions become more intimate. Typically, five minutes will be spent on this discussion.

Second Task:

This is the main activity which should correspond to the theme of the session. Usually, this task lasts about twenty to forty minutes, depending on the length of the total session.

Third Task:

The positive wrap-up of the session is a time for child and therapist to share what they enjoyed about the session. This part usually takes about five minutes.

The components of the above format can be changed, depending on the needs of individual therapists and children.

(6) When working with children, it is essential to have a wide variety of activities, games, books, etc., to use in sessions. Youngsters need a lot of variety, particularly in the first phase of treatment. Please refer to Appendices C and D for suggested materials.

(7) Therapists will need to determine which scales and activities they will use to assess a particular child. A review of any scales recently given to the child should be done to guard against invalid results obtained from a second administration. Sometimes, clinicians will decide on other assessment measures after they begin working with a youngster. More information on the types of scales and activities for assessment of young children will be found later in this chapter.

(8) Learn how to play with children and do not rely so heavily on verbal skills. Clinicians need to meet children at their level of functioning.

(9) Stop what you are doing in sessions if a child does not seem to be responding positively. The therapist will often have to try several approaches for a particular youngster until it is determined which ones are effective.

(10) The therapist should review developmental descriptions of the age child they are working with in therapy. It is essential to know what a typical six-year-old, for example, does, thinks, feels, etc. Only by understanding normal development will the counselor be able to establish realistic expectations for a particular child. Again, Appendix A contains references on child development.

(11) It is usually helpful to obtain impressions of significant others before treatment begins. The opinions of parents and other involved professionals about the child's problems can be quite poignant. Their view of how therapy will benefit a youngster will also be helpful. Readers are referred to the Checklists and Rating Instruments listed in Appendix B as more organized and structured ways of obtaining these observations.

(12) After six to ten sessions, a therapist will usually be ready to complete the assessment and write a report. Sometimes, fewer sessions will be necessary to complete this evaluation.

Assessment Report Form

The reader will find in Table V (Outline for Child Assessment for Individual Therapy) a sample form to follow for assessing a child for individual therapy. This form is simple and straightforward and yet covers all the essential parts of a good assessment report. The report should be limited to two or three pages. It is more practical and helpful to write a concise report that assesses a child's appropriateness for therapy rather than one that attempts to evaluate all areas of functioning. Also, this report should be written so that it can be shared with parents and other involved professionals. Clinicians should only include information in this assessment that they would feel comfortable having family members or other involved professionals read. Readers are referred to a sample assessment report provided in Appendix E.

The Referral section (See Table V) of the assessment report should include the following:

(1) The person(s) making the referral and their reason for this recommendation.

(2) Impressions of the child's major problem areas as seen by significant others. These individuals can include parents, teachers, other counselors, physicians, etc. Clinicians should ask these individuals what they feel would be the benefit of therapy for a particular youngster. Often, families' expectations of treatment can be clearly established here. If their expectations are too unrealistic, then the therapist can address this issue at the end of the assessment when treatment goals are determined. It is recommended that this feedback from others be elicited before treatment begins so the child will see the therapist as his/her counselor exclusively.

(3) Aspects of the child's history may be important if they are directly related to the need for individual therapy and/or the treatment goals. An example of this would be a child's former experience and reaction to individual therapy.

The Description of Child and Session Content section (See Table V) of the assessment report should include the following information.

(1) The number, frequency and duration of assessment sessions that a child attended.

(2) A specific description of the child during the assessment process. It is usually very important to indicate the child's affect, body size/development related to chronological age, physical hygiene, academic level, speech pattern, attention span, contact with reality, memory skills, depth of disclosure and ability to form a beginning relationship with the

TABLE V

OUTLINE FOR CHILD ASSESSMENT FOR INDIVIDUAL THERAPY

Name of Child: _____ Date of Birth: _____

Dates of Assessment: _____

   I. *Referral*

      A. Referral source and reasons
      B. Impressions of significant others
      C. History of child relevant to assessment

  II. *Description of Child and Session Content*

      A. Number and frequency of sessions
      B. Description of child in sessions
      C. Scales and activities administered for assessment purposes

 III. *Assessment Results*

      A. Significant results from scales and assessment activities
      B. Treatment implications from results

 IV. *Treatment Recommendations*

      A. Type of treatment recommended
      B. Rationale for treatment recommended
      C. Treatment goals

Therapist: _____

Date of Report: _____

therapist. This description can sometimes provide more information on a particular child than the results obtained from assessment scales and activities.

(3) A brief summary of the assessment scales and activities used should be included in this section. A listing of these scales and activities appears in Appendix B. It is a good rule of thumb to do at least two objective scales when assessing a child. Informal activities can also be used, but the more objective instruments add validity to a clinician's recommendations. Also, these scales may uncover some problem areas not evident from the assessment activities.

The Assessment Results section (See Table V) of the assessment report should include the following information:

(1) Results gained from the assessment scales and activities administered.

(2) Treatment implications as a result of the significant findings mentioned above. These are the problem areas that will need to be addressed if continued therapy is recommended.

The Treatment Recommendations section (See Table V) of the assessment report should include the following:

(1) The recommendation that individual therapy be continued or discontinued. If the latter is the case, the therapist may want to suggest another more appropriate service such as group therapy, further psychological or psychiatric testing, etc.

(2) The rationale for the recommended service should be clearly stated.

(3) If individual therapy is recommended, the goals for treatment should be provided and established so that they can be attained in about three months of treatment. It will be very important to significant others to know what changes they can expect from a child after a few months of therapy. Goals should be stated with specific behavior changes indicating progress. For example, a possible goal might be stated as follows: To improve the child's self-concept so that (1) he/she is talking more spontaneously in sessions and (2) he/she is more comfortable accepting compliments from the therapist. By stating the goals in this manner, the therapist and significant others will know which changes will indicate treatment progress.

In summary, this assessment report should focus on evaluating a child's appropriateness for individual therapy. Therapists should only indicate history or other impressions in this report that are directly related to this purpose. A sample assessment report found in Appendix E is intended to help the reader further understand the main ingredients of this report. It may be helpful for beginning therapists to use Table V and Appendix E as guides when doing their initial assessments.

A Logging Method for Individual Assessment

Many times therapists will find that the assessment procedure becomes more difficult with the multi-problem child. Sometimes a youngster displays many dysfunctional areas and one is in a dilemma as to where to begin assessment and formulate goals. To this end, a logging method was developed to help make the assessment of complicated cases easier. Even with the less impaired child, this method for collecting and documenting assessment observations and results can be very practical and helpful.

The Log for Individual Therapy Assessment shown in Table VI provides a record for listing significant data sources and findings obtained from administering assessment activities and scales to a child. Feedback and observations from significant others that are obtained through checklists or ratings can also be recorded on this form. A clinician's findings can then be listed in chronological order on this log form. A comprehensive list of evaluative scales and ratings are provided in Appendix B.

Clinicians should review their logs regularly during the assessment process. This review can help determine which scales and activities still need to be implemented. It will also provide ideas on activities that are most effective with a particular child in treatment. Such information can be invaluable for later treatment.

Selection and Use of Assessment Scales

Professionals will find that there are a number of assessment measures for children on the market. Usually, these instruments fall into one of the three categories listed in Appendix B: child scales, ratings/checklists and structured interviews. It is essential that clinicians understand the purpose of each type of scale in order to select appropriate ones for a child's assessment.

The ratings and checklists can be used to obtain data from significant others (i.e., parents, teachers, etc.) regarding the specific problem areas of a youngster. These instruments can also provide a baseline of the child's functioning in other environments prior to individual therapy. Usually, it is best to have these measures completed at the time a client is referred for treatment. Then these same measures can be readministered on a regular basis after therapy begins as a means of measuring

TABLE VI

LOG FOR INDIVIDUAL THERAPY ASSESSMENT

NAME OF CHILD: _____ DATES: _____

SCALES/ACTIVITIES	DATE	SIGNIFICANT FINDINGS
1.		
2.		
3.		
4.		
5.		
6.		
7.		
8.		
9.		
10.		
11.		
12.		

progress. Clinicians will need to determine their own schedule for these readministrations based on their needs and/or those of a particular program.

The child scales are those instruments directly administered to the youngster. Data from these scales provides further specification of a child's problem areas and in some cases establishes an objective baseline of functioning. This information can be used to supplement the data provided from checklists. These measures can be readministered to the child on a regular basis as a way of determining therapeutic progress.

The last type of scale that has only recently come on the market is the structured interview. These instruments not only provide specifics on problem areas of a youngster but also give the clinician specific plans to follow during the assessment sessions. Readers may find these scales most helpful in planning the content of these initial sessions. Some interview forms provide directions as to which behavioral responses in assessment indicate a child's readiness for individual therapy. This assessment measure is one of the few objective instruments that gives some guidelines for determining a child's appropriateness for individual treatment.

Clinicians should remember that there usually is a limit to the amount of assessment data that can be obtained on a child through psychometric instruments alone. Typically, the therapist will know more about a youngster from observations of his/her affect and behavior during the therapeutic play activities in sessions. Sometimes, the primary value of assessment instruments is to add validity to a clinician's impressions and recommendations. Hence, children whose problems are apparent from clinical observations should still have the benefit of formal evaluative measures.

The assessment scales listed in Appendix B are intended to be used by a diverse population of professionals. Such individuals could include psychologists, social workers, psychometricians, psychiatrists, and school counselors. Readers are cautioned, however, that some instruments require specialized training or credentials in order for a clinician to use them. Therapists should always consult the manual of a scale for such information before administering it. In addition, professionals should review thoroughly all the instructions for scale administration provided in this manual.

Clinicians who are working with minority children should review the literature for scales that are sensitive to cultural differences. Also, some instruments have been made available in other languages such as Spanish. As is true for any accurate evaluation, it is essential that a youngster clearly understand the questions and statements presented to him/her. Unless a child is proficient in a second language, it is necessary that the scale be given in one's native language.

As indicated earlier in this chapter, it is recommended that at least two formal scales be administered to each child being seen for an assessment. The reason for this suggestion is the validity added to a report and subsequent recommendation. In addition, these instruments may surface other serious problems or aspects of referral problems that were not evident by informal assessment means (i.e., observations of child in sessions). Usually it is best to select two scales that are evaluating different problem areas of functioning of a child.

Relationship of Activities to the Assessment Procedure

The activities in the following six chapters provide the clinicians with a number of techniques that not only can be used during therapy but also as part of the assessment procedure. In particular, activities found in Chapter Three on Relationship Building/Self-Disclosure can be excellent choices. These activities have been designed to both build a therapeutic relationship and surface problem areas.

Depending on a child's presenting problems, activities from Chapters Four through Seven may be appropriate at this time. Activities in four areas of functioning have been provided in these chapters since they seem to encompass the major aspects of the young child's world: social skills, family, affective awareness and communication, and school. Other more pervasive problems such as depression or low self-esteem can be treated through the activity areas where such issues surface. For example, if a child is usually depressed at home, specific activities from Chapter Five "Activities Related to Family" can be used to increase his/her awareness of this problem and to provide some alternatives for coping.

After the assessment is completed, the therapist will use this treatment plan to determine which activity chapters are most appropriate. For example, if it is found that treatment for a particular youngster needs to focus on expressing feelings at home, activities from Chapters Four, "Activities Related to Affective Awareness and Communication," and Six, "Activities Related to Family," would be most appropriate for this child.

If a therapist finds that a problem area is not addressed in one of these four activity chapters, then he/she will have to develop therapeutic interventions focusing on that area. Readers are referred to Appendix C for references on others sources for planning ideas. The activities in this book should provide examples of the types of therapeutic games that can be utilized. Clinicians can then change the content of those activities to address the more relevant problem area(s) of the youngster.

Summary

The primary purpose of this chapter is to provide a guide for setting up, planning, and facilitating assessment sessions. An assessment report form with a method of logging data collection and findings is outlined to give structure and goal focus to this evaluative procedure. Therapists will find that a formal assessment will assist in determining the most appropriate type of treatment and the individualization of the treatment plan. The end result will be a higher probability of significant therapeutic impact.

CHAPTER THREE

ACTIVITIES RELATED TO RELATIONSHIP BUILDING/SELF-DISCLOSURE

IN THIS CHAPTER, the reader will find activities related to the areas of relationship building and self-disclosure. The therapist should always use these or similar activities when beginning treatment with a child.

As indicated by their title, these activities assist the clinician in building a trusting relationship with the client. At the same time, these games help the child to gradually open up in therapy. Professionals will find that some activities in this chapter will address the self-concept of the child and can be used to address problems in that area of functioning.

A listing of the themes addressed by the activities in this chapter are found on Table VII, Themes for Activities Related to Relationship Building/Self-Disclosure. Clinicians can use this table as a guide for selecting appropriate interventions with children who are in the first phase of therapy.

TABLE VII
THEMES FOR RELATIONSHIP BUILDING/SELF-DISCLOSURE ACTIVITIES

PAGE	ACTIVITY	THEME
32	"My Face" Completion	Child's perception of his face
33	"My Face" Completion	
34	Follow the Dots	Child's perception of his body
35	Opposites Game	
36	"My Five Senses" Completion	Sensory awareness of child
37	Guess Which Sense!	
38	"My Family" Picture Completion	Child's perception of his/her family
39	"My Family" Tree	Child's familiarity with extended family
40	"My Home" Completion	Exploring child's home environment
41	Computer Fill-in	
42	Pet Word Completion	Child's feelings about pets
43	Pet Name Game	
44	Morning Time Multiple Choice	Exploring child's wake-up behavior
45	Morning Time Completion	
46	Nighttime Completion	Child's perception of bedtime needs
47	Nighttime Fill-in	
48	Talking Time Fill-in	Exploring child's needs for talking
49	Talking Time Opposites Game	
50	Birthday Cake Word Search	Child's awareness of growth and change with age
51	Birthday Card Fill-in	
52	"Special Things I Can Do" Matching	Child's perception of his/her special talents
53	"Special Things I Can Do" Rebus Puzzle	

TABLE VII *(continued)*

THEMES FOR RELATIONSHIP BUILDING/SELF-DISCLOSURE ACTIVITIES

PAGE	ACTIVITY	THEME
54	Hidden Pictures	Games child likes to play
55	Games Word Scramble	
56	T.V. Picture Completion	Child's T.V. watching behavior
57	T.V. Code Game	
58	"Me and My Clothes" Completion	Exploring child's view on his/her clothing
59	"My Clothes" Fill-in	
60	Awards Fill-in	Child's experience with times of recognition
61	Awards Word Search	
62	"My Good Days" Completion	Child's perception of his/her good days and desirable awards
63	Good Days Ladder	Child's perception of his/her good days
64	"When I Get Into Trouble" Completion	Child's awareness of his/her times of getting into trouble
65	Coded Message	
66	Word Completion	Ways someone can show care and concern to the child
67	Thank You Card	
68	"I Wish I Were. . ." Photograph	Child's perception of whom he/she would like to be
69	Ideal Person Program	
70	Future Looks Game	Exploring child's hopes for his/her body attributes as an adult
71	Sentence Maze	Exploring child's feelings about his/her special body features
72	"What I Need" Robot Fill-in	Child's perception of his/her present needs
73	"What I Need" Completion	

"My Face" Completion

 "Here is a drawing of my face . . ."

Now color in all the parts of your face that make you a unique being including:

1. Curly, wavy, or straight hair.
2. Hair color
3. Eye color
4. Freckles
5. Missing Teeth
6. Other

"My Face" Completion

"Here is a drawing of my face..."

[drawing box]

1. "I think my face is _____
   _____
   _____."

2. I like this part of my face the best.
   ☐ my eyes   ☐ my hair
   ☐ my nose   ☐ my teeth
   ☐ my mouth   ☐ my ears

3. The part of my face I would like
   to change is _____.

4. People say I have a nice looking
   face.
   ☐ yes
   ☐ no

Follow the Dots

Draw a line connecting the dots to make an earthling body.

```
                      13
              12.   ·    14
                         ·

           11·              ·15

           10·              ·16

              9.       ·17

           7.  8.     ·18
                          ·19
         6.                   ·20

                               ·21

      5.   43               ·22
                    31·
         4,                      ·23
                              30·
      3·    ·44

  START                                    ·24
  HERE   2                               ·    ·25
     1   ·    42        32           29·
         ·                         28·    ·26
      ·45                  37         ·27
      ·46
  48·
     47
```

```
              41
     40.   ·              33·
                              ·34
   39·     38·    36·       ·35
```

Now color in the features that make you a unique earthling:

1. Hair color   4. Skin color

2. Eye color   5. Any characteristic,
                            clothing or object

3. Special body markings
```
```

Opposites Game

Draw a line between the words that are opposites. All these words have to do with features of people's bodies. Circle the ones that apply to you.

right handed	straight
thin	light
tall	clumsy
handsome	undeveloped
curly	healthy
slow	fat
dark	left handed
coordinated	short
sick	fast
developed	unattractive

"My Five Senses" Completion

This extraterrestrial creature wants to learn about your five senses.

Fill in the blanks below to describe your favorite things.

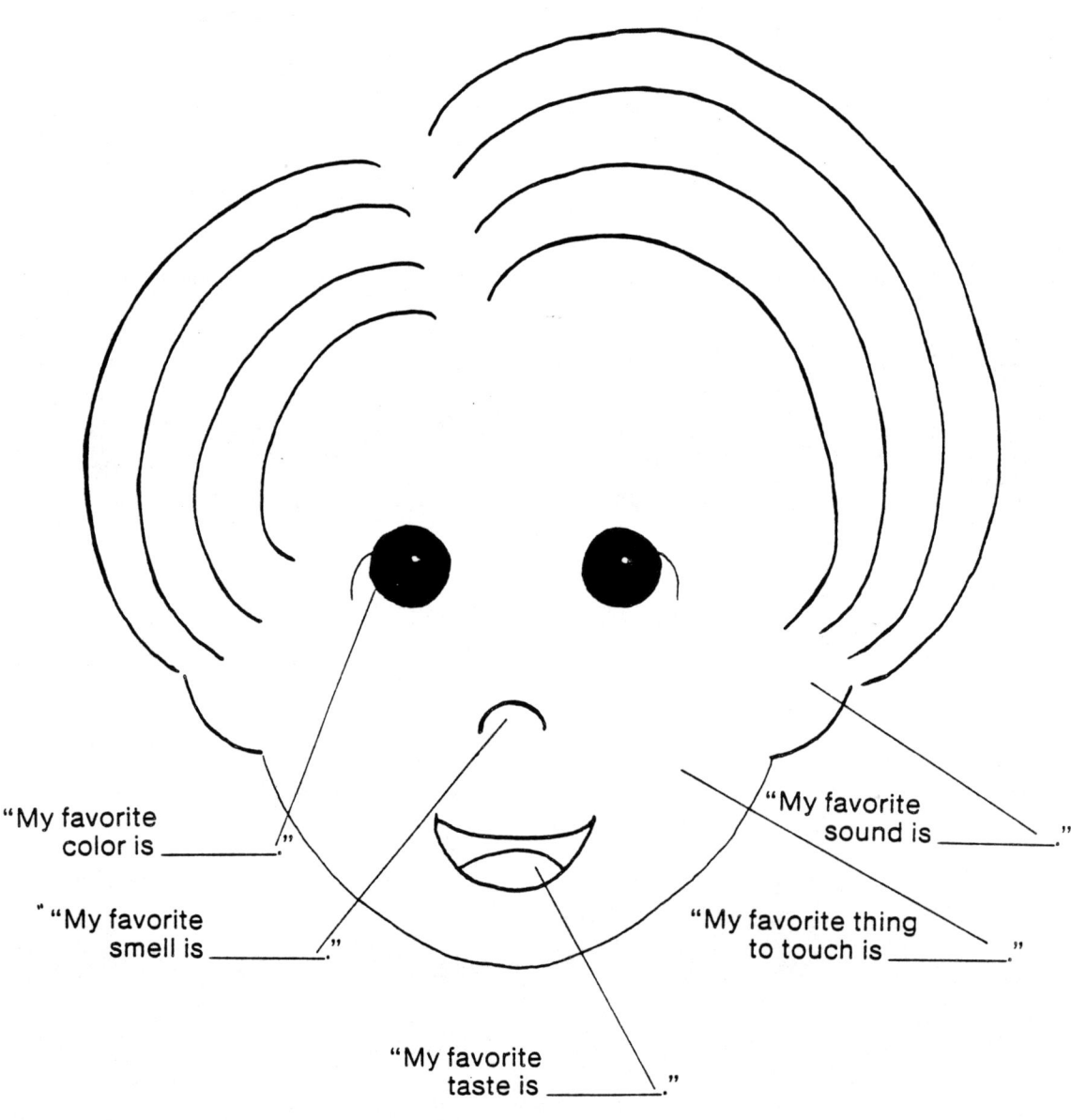

"My favorite color is _____."

" "My favorite smell is _____."

"My favorite sound is _____."

"My favorite thing to touch is _____."

"My favorite taste is _____."

Guess Which Sense!

Fill in the boxes with the number of the sense you use to identify each of the 14 qualities below. Some items may have more than one answer.

1	2	3	4	5
eyes	ears	nose	mouth	hands

1. Red ☐ ☐ ☐	8. Furry	☐ ☐ ☐
2. Sour ☐ ☐ ☐	9. Hard	☐ ☐ ☐
3. Loud ☐ ☐ ☐	10. Gentle	☐ ☐ ☐
4. Quiet ☐ ☐ ☐	11. Cold	☐ ☐ ☐
5. Hot ☐ ☐ ☐	12. Sharp	☐ ☐ ☐
6. Salty ☐ ☐ ☐	13. Sweet	☐ ☐ ☐
7. Soft ☐ ☐ ☐	14. Rough	☐ ☐ ☐

"My Family" Picture Completion

Draw a picture of all your family members doing something together in your house.

"My Family Tree"

Fill in the names of your family members. If you have brothers or sisters, write their ages, too.

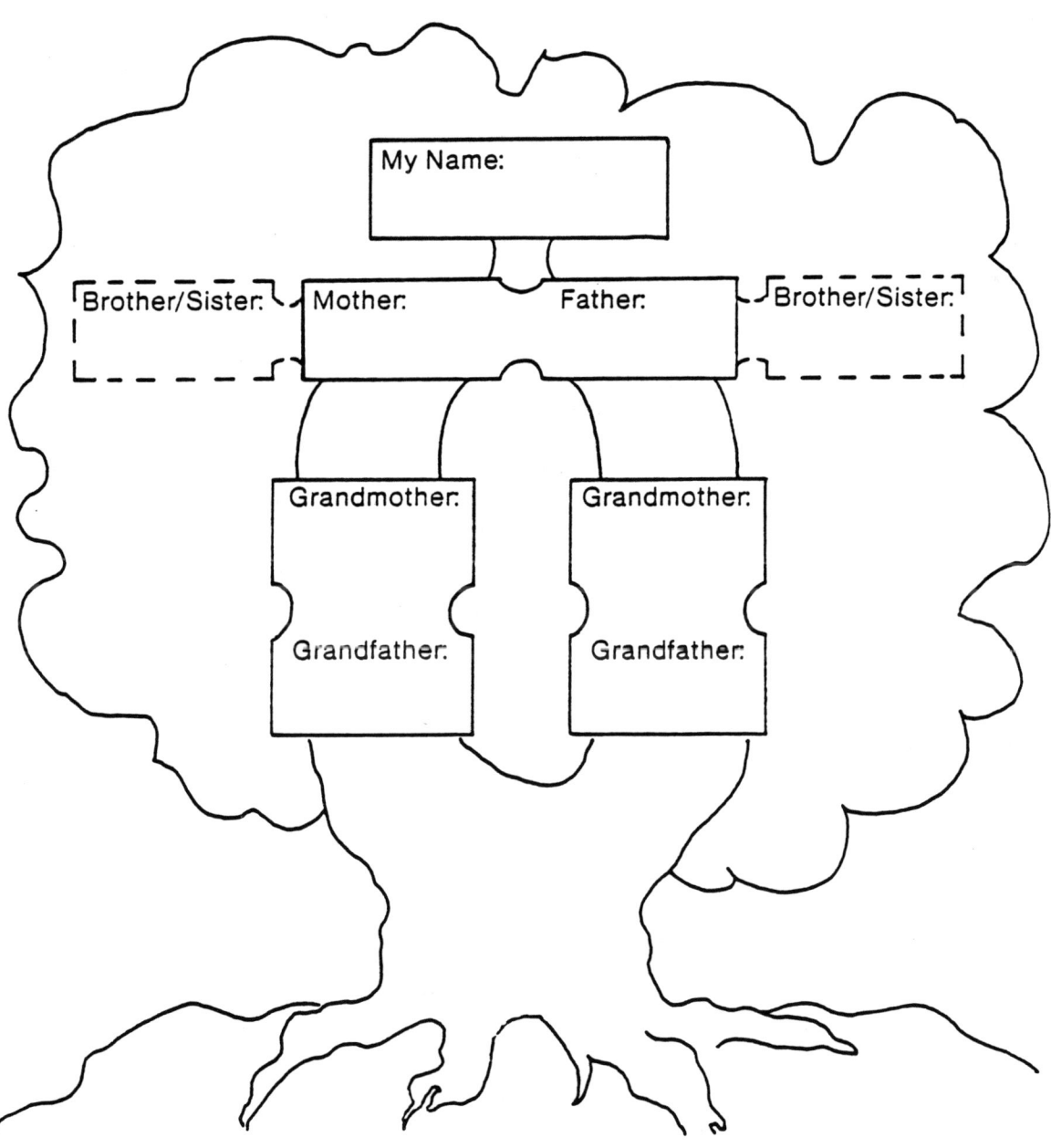

My Name:

Brother/Sister: Mother: Father: Brother/Sister:

Grandmother: Grandmother:

Grandfather: Grandfather:

"My Home" Completion

 Complete the following:

1. "I live in..."

   ☐ a house

   ☐ a mobile home

   ☐ an apartment building

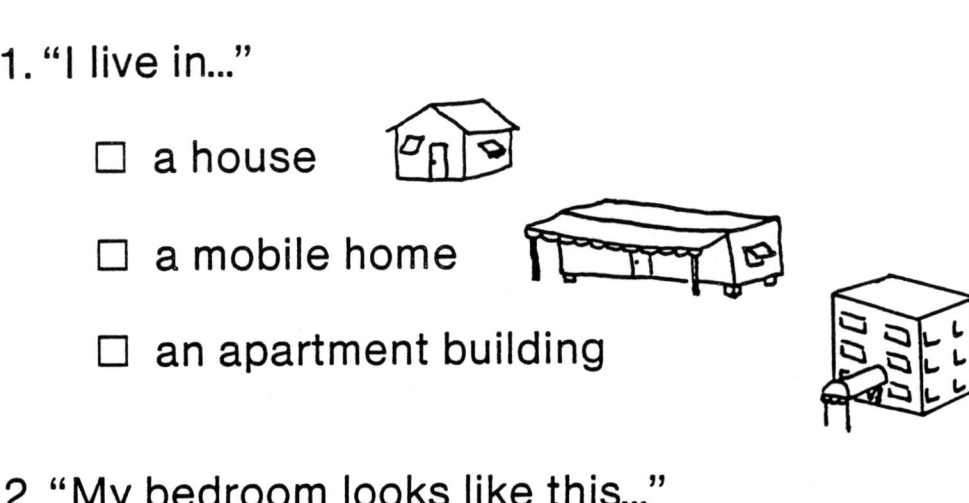

2. "My bedroom looks like this..."

   a. Cut out the numbers of beds in your room and place them as they appear.

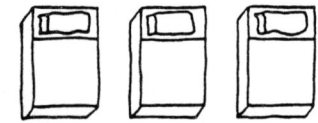

   b. Draw in doors, windows, bathrooms as they appear.

   c. Draw in any other furniture as it appears (desk, toybox, etc.)

Computer Fill-In

Enter the data that best describes your home in the computer.

1. I live in a _____.
2. We have ____ bedrooms and ____ bathrooms at home.
3. I share my bedroom with_____.
4. My favorite room at home is _____.
5. The best thing about our home is _____.
6. I think our house is _____ for my family.
7. One thing I would like to change about our house is _____.

Pet Word Completion

Finish drawing these animals that live on the planet earth and write what they are called in the blanks provided.

— — — — —

— — — —

— — — —

— — — — —

"My favorite animal is a _____."

"I have this animal as a pet. ☐ Yes ☐ No"

Pet Name Game

Write down all the pets you can think of in 3 minutes. The player with the most pets wins game number one. For game number two, each player tries to remember the pets on their opponent's list. Players may look at each other's list for 10 seconds beforehand.

Player: _____

1. _____
2. _____
3. _____
4. _____
5. _____
6. _____
7. _____
8. _____
9. _____
10. _____

Player: _____

1. _____
2. _____
3. _____
4. _____
5. _____
6. _____
7. _____
8. _____
9. _____
10. _____

Morning Time Multiple Choice

Put a check in the box that best answers the following:

1. "Getting up in the morning is ☐ hard
☐ easy."

2. "I wake up in the morning ☐ by myself
☐ with an alarm clock
☐ with someone's help."

3. "When I get up, I usually feel ☐ tired
☐ grumpy
☐ afraid
☐ happy."

Color in your favorite breakfast in the drawing below:

Morning Time Completion

 Complete the following sentences:

1. Astronauts sleep buckled up in a compartment bed. Where do you sleep? "I sleep _____."

2. Astronauts wake up by a digital alarm clock. How do you wake up? "I wake up _____."

3. It is always dark outside when astronauts wake up. What is it like outside when you wake up? "It is _____."

4. Astronauts have freeze-dried eggs & toast for breakfast. What do you eat for breakfast?
   "I _____."

5. Sometimes an astronaut wakes up on the "wrong side of the space shuttle." How do you feel when you wake up?" I feel _____
   _____."

Nighttime Completion

Put a check in the box and fill in the sentences to describe your bedtime.

1. "Before I go to bed at night, I like it the most when someone:

☐ Gives me a snack   ☐ Reads to me

☐ Has a private talk   ☐ Tucks me into bed"
with me

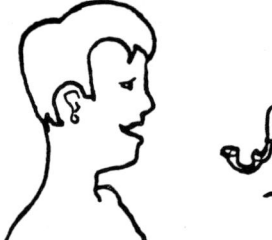 

2. "Sometimes I have trouble getting to sleep ☐ yes ☐ no"

3. "My bed time is _____ o'clock."

4. "Some of the dreams I remember having are _____
_____
_____."

Nighttime Fill-In

Imagine that you are older and are babysitting for another child your real age. Design a plan that would make an ideal evening/bedtime for that child.

Babysitter Plan for the Evening

Bedtime will be at _____.

Before the child goes to bed I will make sure he
_____.

Some things we will do for fun before bedtime are
_____.

The best snack before bed would be _____.

If the child has trouble getting to sleep I will
_____.

Planned by: _____
                         Your Signature

Talking Time Fill-In

✏️ Complete this notice for your bedroom door so your family will know the best time to talk with you.

Notice to my Family

"Please remember to talk with me _____.

When I feel _____, please do talk to me.

When I feel _____, please do not talk to me. I

think it is important to talk about _____. I

particularly like to talk with _____. I wish I

could talk to _____ more."

Talking Time Opposites Game

Draw a line between the words that are opposites. All these words have to do with times when you like to talk. Circle the ones that apply to you.

morning	after school
before school	weekdays
always	never
doing	happy
upset	resting
good behavior	school
weekends	night
home	bad behavior

Birthday Cake Word Search

See how many times you can find the word "birthday" among the letters on the cake and circle them.

Draw the number of candles that you will have on your next birthday cake.

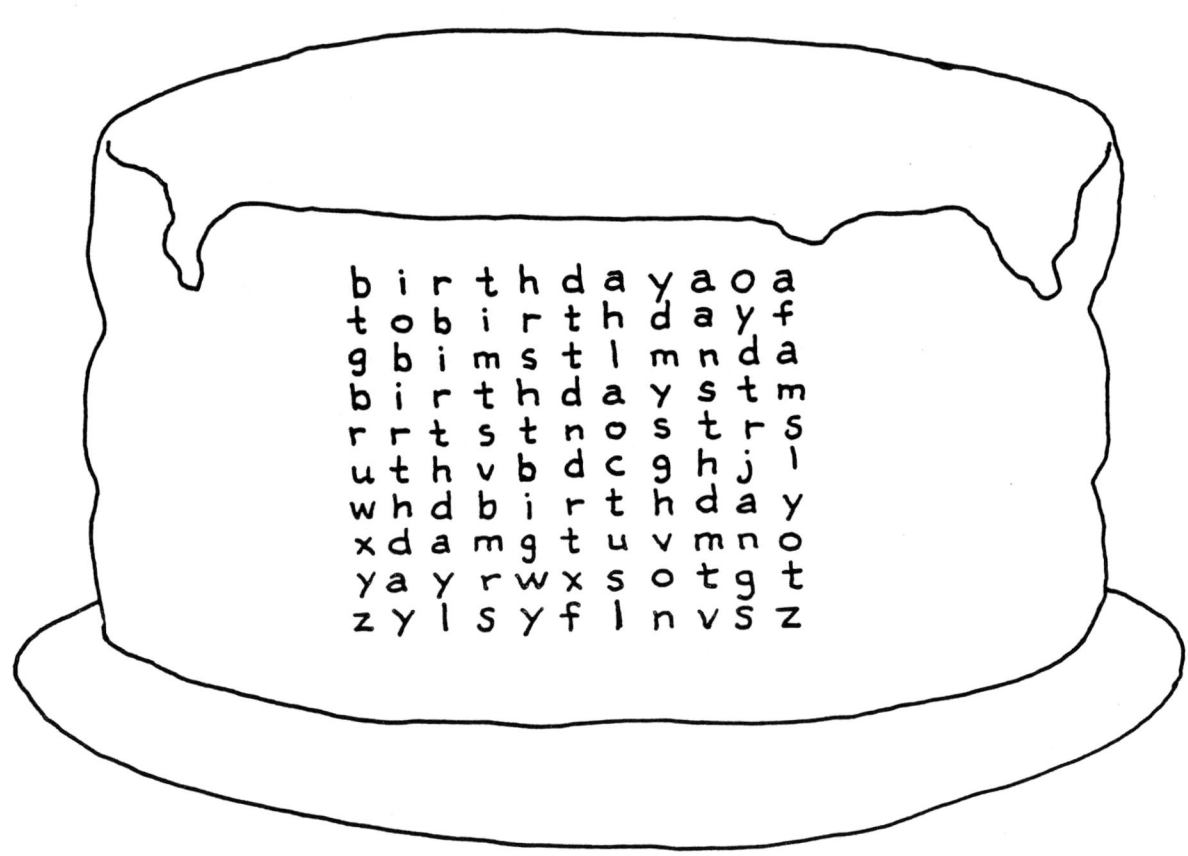

Write one new thing that you have learned this year _____.

Birthday Card Fill-In

 Write a birthday card to yourself indicating all the new things you can do since your last birthday.

Birthdate:

HAPPY
BIRTHDAY
TO

Now that I am a year
older I am able to:

This birthday should be ☐ The best yet
☐ OK
☐ Not so good

"Special Things I Can Do" Matching

 Connect the picture that goes with each word below.

Reading

Arts and Crafts

Skiing

Ball Games

Playing an instrument

Swimming

Dancing

Singing

Color the picture that is your favorite thing to do. Write or draw it here if it is not included.

"Special Things I Can Do" Rebus Puzzle

Add or subtract the letters and the pictures to come up with special things you can do.

[saw] −aw + [witch] −tch + [mop] −op =	[dog] −og + [pan] −p + [face] −fa =
[strainer] −ope + [cup] −t + [door] −oor =	[daisy] −aisy + [rain] −in + [bird] −atch =
[bread] −red + [lad] −do [xylophone] −te + [frames] −fr =	[muscle] −cle + [stick] −stk =

Circle the one that is your special thing to do. Write it here if it is not included above. _____.

Hidden Pictures
Robot Birthday Party

In the big picture, find these games and circle them.

"My favorite kind of playing is _____."
"I play my favorite game ☐ with others
                          ☐ by myself."

Games Word Scramble

Unscramble the following words that have to do with games you can play. Circle the one you like to play the best.

1. blal gmase _____

2. drooin gsame _____

3. urninng gmeas _____

4. ardwning _____

5. erpetend gmaes _____

6. kibe dinrig _____

7. obadr gmaes _____

8. racd mgase _____

T.V. Picture Completion

Write or Draw your favorite T.V. show on this television screen.

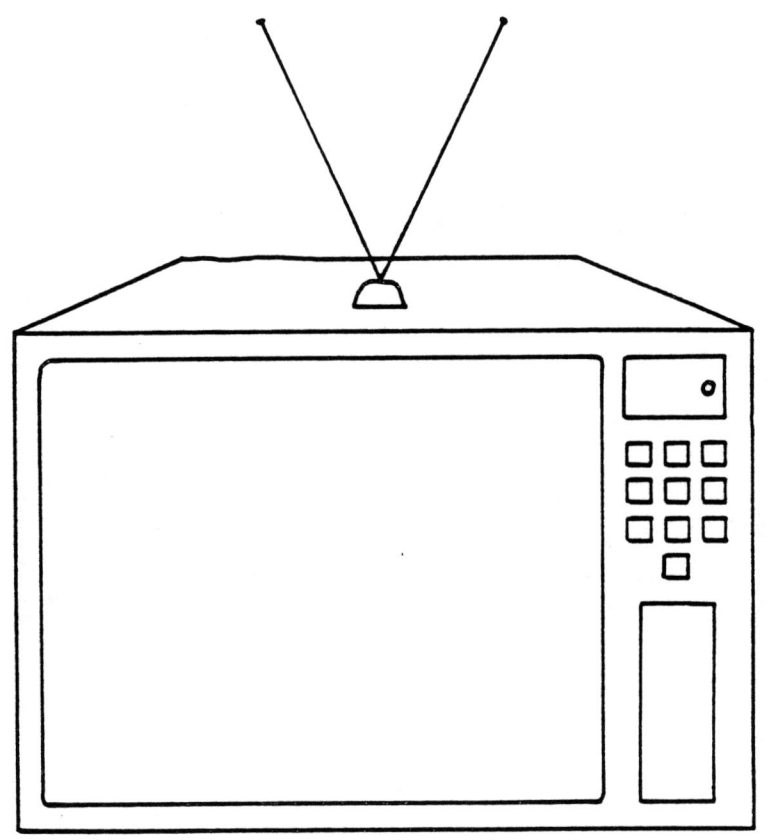

"I watch T.V.
- ☐ all the time
- ☐ sometimes
- ☐ never."

What we see on T.V. is
- ☐ always true
- ☐ sometimes true
- ☐ almost never true

T.V. Code Game

✏ Use the code below to spell out this important message!

1	2	3	4	5	6	7	8	9	10	11	12	13	14	15	16	17	18	19	20	21	22	23	24	25	26
A	B	C	D	E	F	G	H	I	J	K	L	M	N	O	P	Q	R	S	T	U	V	W	X	Y	Z

"9•20   9•19   9•13•16•15•18•20•1•14•20

— —   — —   — — — — — — — —

20•15   20•8•9•14•11   1•2•15•21•20

— —   — — — — —   — — — — —

23•8•1•20   25•15•21   19•5•5   15•14

— — — —   — — —   — — —   — —

20•22   1•14•4   4•5•3•9•4•5   9•6

— —   — — —   — — — — — —   — —

9•20   9•19   20•18•21•5."

— —   — —   — — — —

"My favorite T.V. show is _____."

57

"Me and My Clothes" Completion

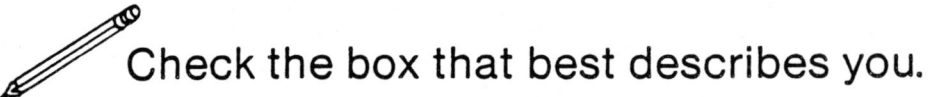 Check the box that best describes you.

1. "I pick out my own clothes to wear
   in the morning ☐ yes
             ☐ no."

2. "I help select my own clothes when I
   go shopping ☐ yes
           ☐ sometimes
           ☐ never."

3. "My clothes are very important to me ☐ yes
                                   ☐ no."

4. "The best kind of clothing to buy for me is _____."

"My Clothes" Fill-In

Make a shopping list of all the clothes and shoes you would like to buy with the approximate cost next to each item.

Clothing Shopping List

Item   Cost

_____   _____

_____   _____

_____   _____

_____   _____

_____   _____

_____   _____

_____   _____

_____   _____

Total Cost: _____

Awards Fill-In

 Complete the following:

1. "When awards are given out, I...
   - ☐ often get one
   - ☐ sometimes get one
   - ☐ never get one."

2. "The best award I ever got was _____."

3. "I think I deserve an award for..."
   (fill in the award)

```
┌─────────────────────────────────────┐
│                                      │
│      _____     │
│                                      │
│      _____     │
│                                      │
│                                      │
│      _____      🎖     │
│                                      │
└─────────────────────────────────────┘
```

Enjoying what you do is a far greater reward.
What do you think?

Awards Word Search

Circle all the words that are ways you could win an award. See if you can find all 12.

Now circle in red the ways you have received an award. Write your name on the award in your best handwriting.

This is to certify that _____ has won an award for...

```
r u n n i n g r s t t
f e t r a m m a t h r
s o s d a n c e u s a
p f o o t b a l l q c
e s c f r e a d i n g
l c c b a s e b a l l
l i e a n o m a s o s
i e r s i n g i n g m
n n n i f a c a e y m
g c o c t e i n r e g
g e p s m p c f s t f
```

"My Good Days" Completion

Someone has just given you a gift for having a week of all good days. Draw or write what should be in this box for you. How did you earn it?

Good Days Ladder

Write down on the rungs of this ladder all the words or phrases that have to do with ways you have had good days. See if you can reach the top.

"When I Get Into Trouble" Completion

Check the answer that fits for you.

1. "I usually get into trouble when...
   ☐ I am by myself.
   ☐ I am with others."

2. "When I get into trouble at home...
   ☐ I cannot watch T.V.
   ☐ I have to go to my room.
   ☐ I get a spanking.
   ☐ Other _____."

3. "The punishment I usually get is...
   ☐ Fair.
   ☐ Unfair."

4. "I get into trouble...
   ☐ Once in awhile.
   ☐ All the time."

Coded Message

Fill in the missing word in this message. To decode the missing word, cross out all the letters that appear twice among the group of letters.

T O G A R S B M
S G A L M N E U N

Everyone gets into _____ every once in awhile.

"I get into trouble...
☐ once in awhile
☐ all the time."

"The punishment I usually get is...
☐ fair.
☐ unfair."

How can you learn from your mistakes?

Word Completion

Complete the following sentences by filling in the missing letters to the incomplete words.

"I like it when someone...

...gives me a h __ __."

...k__ __ __ __ s me."

...r__ __ __ s to me."

...gives me a tr__ __ t."

...gives me a g__ __ __."

...says something n__ __ __ to me."

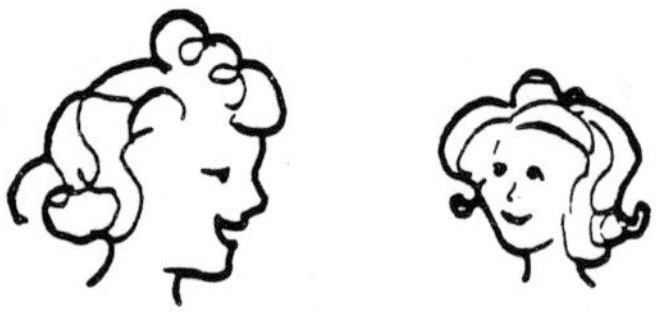

How do other people know
what you like?

66

Thank You Card

Cut out and complete this thank you card to someone who has done something nice for you recently.

Dear _____,

Thank you for

_____

_____

_____

_____

Love,

"I Wish I were..." Photograph

Pretend you just took a picture of the person that you wish you could be. Draw this photograph & write the name of the person on the label.

Would you be a lot happier if you were this person?

☐Yes
☐No

Ideal Person Program

Program into this computer a profile of the ideal person.

Looks like _____

Does school work like _____

Plays games like _____

Is a good friend like _____

Has a family like _____

Would you be a lot happier if you were this ideal person? ☐ Yes
☐ No

Future Looks Game

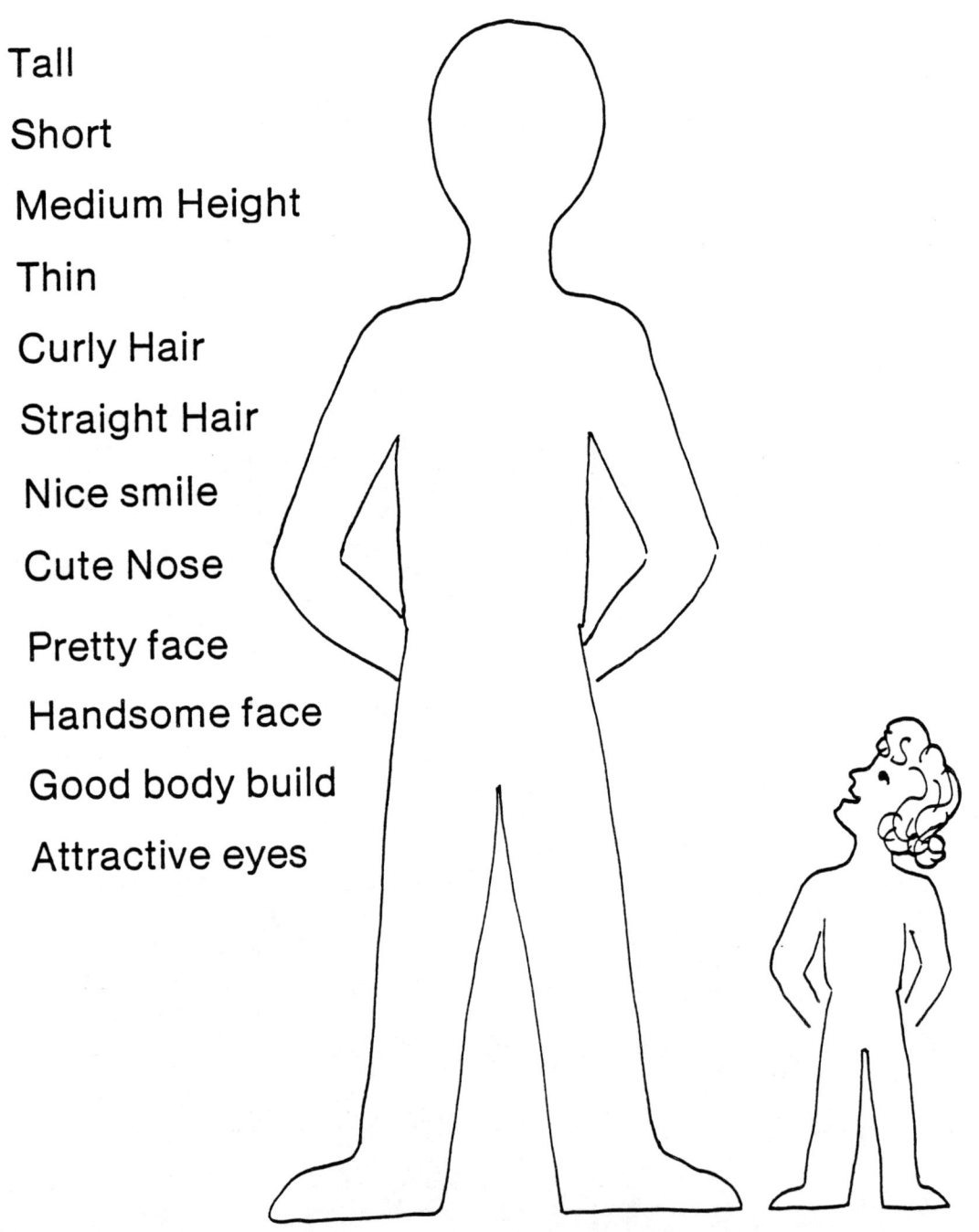

Circle the words that describe how you hope you look when you grow up. Feel free to complete the drawing of yourself in the future.

Tall

Short

Medium Height

Thin

Curly Hair

Straight Hair

Nice smile

Cute Nose

Pretty face

Handsome face

Good body build

Attractive eyes

Sentence Maze

Follow the path that spells out the message about our looks.

"What I Need" Robot Fill-In

Imagine that this robot is going to take care of all your needs. Program it for this job.

"At home I need for you to _____.

At school help me to _____.

When I am upset _____.

Always be sure to _____."

How can you take care of your needs?

"What I Need" Completion

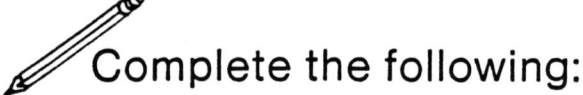Complete the following:

1. "At school I need to...
   - ☐ Have more friends.
   - ☐ Do better work.
   - ☐ Get along better with my teachers."

2. "At home I need to...
   - A. Get along better with my family.
   - B. Help around the house more.
   - C. Play better in my neighborhood.
   - D. Other _____."

3. "What I need from others is...
   - ☐ More attention.
   - ☐ More hugs.
   - ☐ More help.
   - ☐ Other _____."

How can you take care of your needs?

CHAPTER FOUR

ACTIVITIES RELATED TO AFFECTIVE AWARENESS AND COMMUNICATION

IN THIS CHAPTER, the reader will find activities related to the awareness and communication of feelings. Children who are withdrawn, depressed, angry and acting out, or extremely upset over a crisis in their life will be the types of clients to benefit from these activities. These activities should be used in the middle phase of therapy.

A listing of the themes addressed by the activities in this chapter can be found in Table VIII, Themes for Activities Related to Affective Awareness and Communication. Readers can use this table as a guide for selecting an appropriate intervention to use with a child who is working on affective skills in treatment.

TABLE VIII
THEMES FOR AFFECTIVE AWARENESS AND COMMUNICATION ACTIVITIES

PAGE	ACTIVITY	THEME
78	Feelings Word Jumble	Identifying different feelings
79	Feelings Game	
80	"Feeling Happy to Me is. . ."	Exploring sources of happiness for a child
81	Crossword Puzzle	
82	Happy Face Match Up	Exploring people with whom the child feels happy
83	Word Find	Exploring situations where the child is happy
84	"Feeling Sad to Me is. . ."	Body awareness of feeling sad
85	Crossword Puzzle	Identifying times when a child feels sad
86	"Feeling Angry to Me is. . ."	Body awareness of feeling angry
87	How Angry? Multiple Choice	Exploring child's intensity of anger in various situations
88	"Feeling Afraid to Me is. . ."	Body awareness of feeling afraid
89	Opposites Game	Identifying times that bring on afraid feelings
90	"Feeling Proud to Me is. . ."	Body awareness of feeling proud
91	Hidden Word Game	Identifying sources of proud feelings
92	"Feeling Lonely" Crossword Puzzle	Exploring times a child feels lonely
93	"Feeling Lonely" Letter Association	
94	"Feeling Excited" Multiple Choice	Awareness of child's responses to feeling excited
95	"Feeling Excited" Story Completion	Awareness of a situation that would bring on excited feelings

TABLE VIII *(continued)*

THEMES FOR AFFECTIVE AWARENESS AND COMMUNICATION ACTIVITIES

PAGE	ACTIVITY	THEME
96	"Feeling Frustrated" Sentence Completion	Exploring how a child likes to deal with frustrated feelings
97	"Feeling Frustrated" Secret Code	
98	"Feeling Smart" Matching	Identifying academic subjects in which a child feels smart
99	"Feeling Smart" Completion	Exploring how a child feels smart
100	"Feeling Bored" Picture Completion	Identifying ways to stop feeling bored
101	"My Bored Feelings"	Identifying times when a child feels bored
102	"Being Tired" Picture Completion	Facial awareness of being tired
103	"Being Tired" Opposites Game	Identifying times when a child is tired
104	"My Feelings at Home"	Identifying feelings a child experiences at home
105	"At Home" Feelings Chart	Identifying usual feelings of family members
106	"My Feelings with Mom and Dad"	Identifying full range of feelings experienced with parents
107	"My Feelings with Mom and Dad"	
108	"My Feelings with Friends"	Identifying feelings experienced with friends
109	Coded Message	
110	"My Feelings at School"	Identifying causes of various feelings at school
111	"My Feelings at School"	
112	Hidden Word Game	Conveying to child realistic expectations of friendship
113	Code Game	Learning how feelings are felt not controlled

Feelings Word Jumble

This little space creature wants to learn about **all** your different feelings. Find the following words in this letter jumble and make each one a different color: HAPPY, SAD, ANGRY, EXCITED, AFRAID, LONELY, TIRED, PROUD, FRUSTRATED, EMBARRASSED, SURPRISED, BORED, GUILTY, HURT, O.K.

Feelings Game

Cut out the two score sheets below. Each player should write down as many feelings as they can in 3 minutes. The player with the longest list wins.

Player _____	Player _____
1. _____	1. _____
2. _____	2. _____
3. _____	3. _____
4. _____	4. _____
5. _____	5. _____
6. _____	6. _____
7. _____	7. _____
8. _____	8. _____
9. _____	9. _____
10. _____	10. _____

"Feeling Happy To Me Is..."

 1. When this space creature is feeling happy, his feelers are pink and they glow. Color them.

2. "When I am feeling happy, this is the way I look."

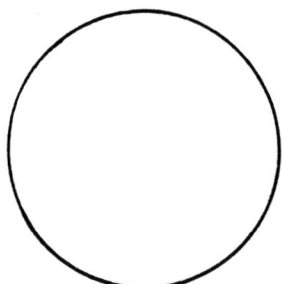

3. Name three things that usually make you happy.

_____

_____

_____

Who really makes you happy?
You, or others?

80

Crossword Puzzle

Complete the crossword puzzle and help this space creature to learn what earthlings do when they are happy.

Down

1. A happy face has a _ _ _ _ _.

3. When something is funny we _ _ _ _ _.

4. When we want to look at people, we keep our eyes _ _ _ _.

6. It's fun to _ _ _ _ with your toys.

Across

2. When we're happy our eyes _ _ _ _ _ _ _.

5. Sometimes we feel like _ _ _ _ _ _ _ up and down.

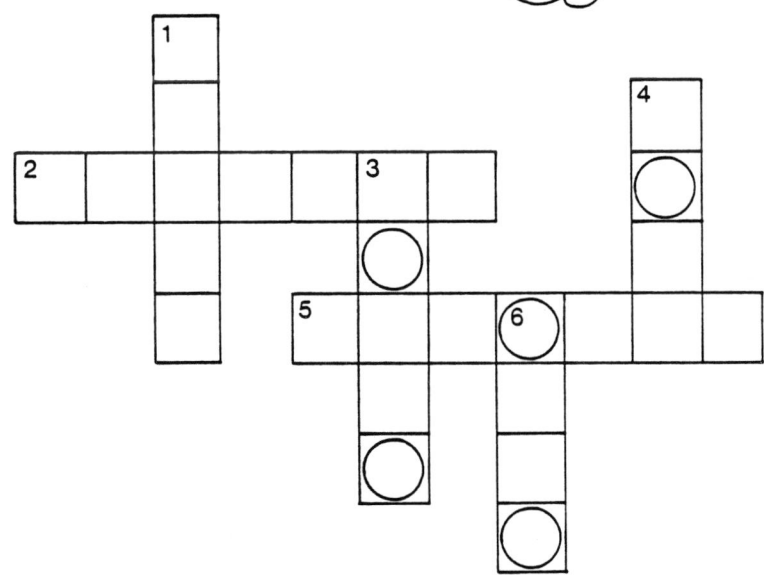

What word do the circled letters spell?

_ _ _ _ _

Happy Face Match Up

Draw a line from this happy face to where you feel happy most often. Now color the faces that you connected to the happy face.

"With my friends"

"With adults"

"By Myself"

Being happy by yourself is a good thing. What do you think?

Word Find

Circle all the words below that have to do with people, places, and experiences that make you feel happy. See if you can find all eight.

```
f r i e n d s a f e c
a a p g b h r s h g i
m u s i c o r t s b t
i u t u e m y s e l f
l o v e f e m x y m n
t y j g a m e s p z o
f t s c h o o l n o f
```

"Feeling Sad To Me Is..."

When this space creature is feeling sad, his feelers, have no life. They are blue & wilted. Color them.

"When I am feeling sad, I can feel it...
(Color the body below)

a. in my eyes
b. in my speech/voice
c. in my body

d. in my stomach
e. in the way I walk
f. other."

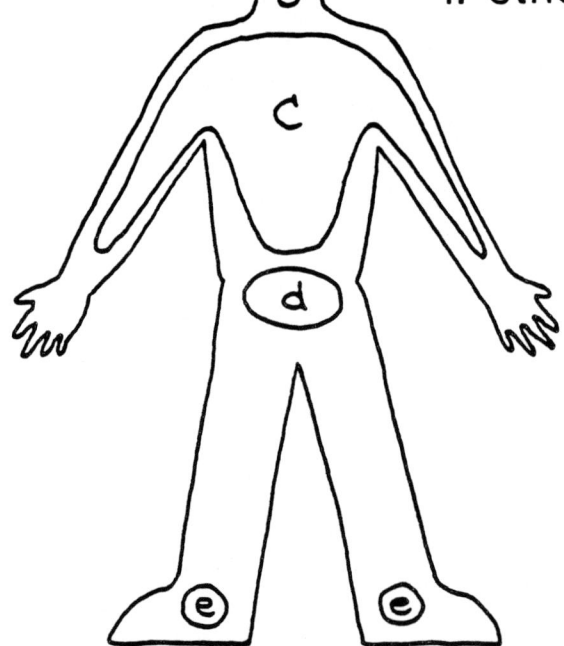

What could you do about those sad feelings?

Crossword Puzzle

Complete this crossword puzzle with words that have to do with feeling sad.

Across

1. By oneself
3. Gone forever
5. Bruised
6. Tears

Down

2. Go to a different house; leave
3. Not married any longer
5. Strike
7. Scream

"Feeling Angry To Me Is..."

When this space creature is feeling angry, his feelers are red hot. Color them.

"When I am feeling angry, I can feel it...
(color the body below)

a. in my head
b. in my speech/voice
c. in my body

d. in my stomach
e. in the way I use
   my hands/feet
f. other

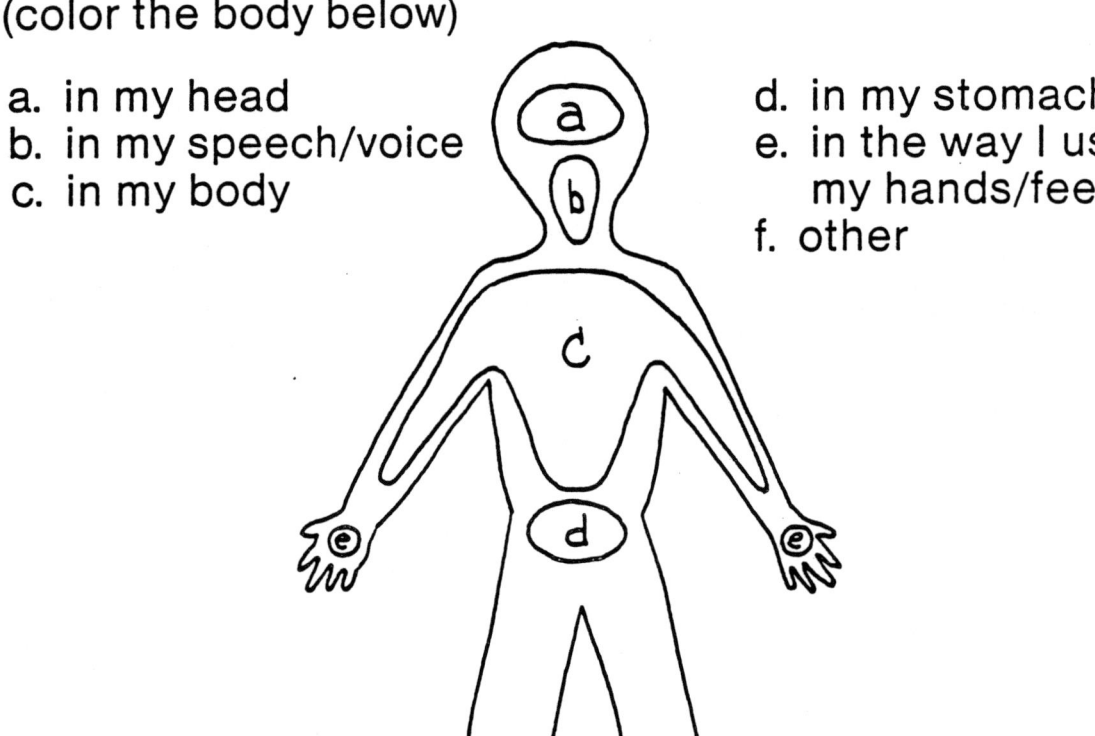

How do you take care of those angry feelings?

86

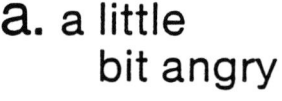 # How Angry? Multiple Choice

Complete the sentences by filling in the letter that fits the best for you.

 **a.** a little
bit angry

 **b.** pretty
angry

 **c.** very
angry

d. other

1. "When I am wrongly accused of doing something, I feel _____."
2. "When someone takes one of my toys without permission, I feel _____."
3. "When an adult yells at me, I feel _____."
4. "Sometimes we get _____ with friends that we like the most."
5. "It frightens me when someone else is _____."
6. Every once in awhile, its O.K. to feel _____ . It's a good idea to learn to take care of that anger.

How do you prevent yourself from getting too angry?

"Feeling Afraid To Me Is..."

 1. When this space creature is feeling afraid, his feelers shake and are cold. Color them gray.

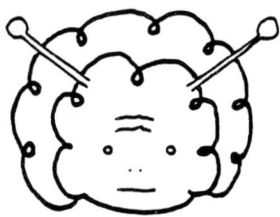

2. "When I am feeling afraid, I can feel it... (color the body below)

a. in my head
b. in my speech/voice
c. in my body

 d. in my stomach
e. in my hands
f. other

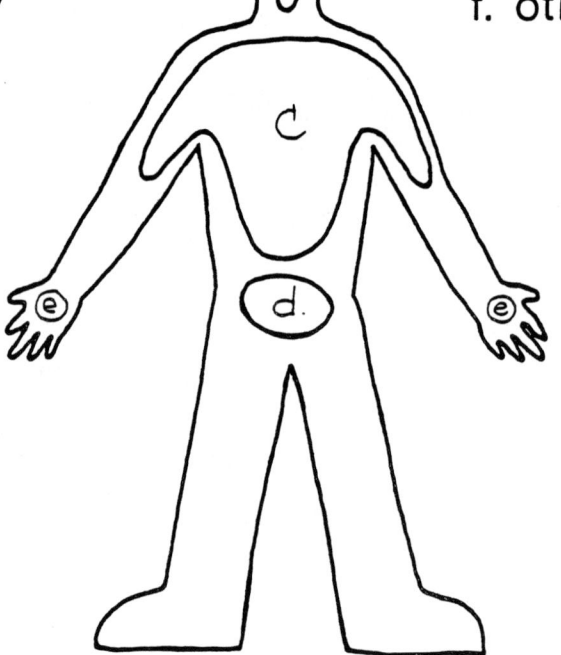

How can you become less afraid?

Opposites Game

Draw a line between the words that are opposites. All these words have to do with times you might feel afraid. Circle the ones that apply to you.

dark	sick
yelling	day
play	dad
alone	small
healthy	punishment
night	light
kids	together
mom	quiet
big	work
reward	adults

"Feeling Proud To Me Is..."

When this space creature feels proud, his feelers stand straight & tall, and they sparkle.

"This is me feeling proud."

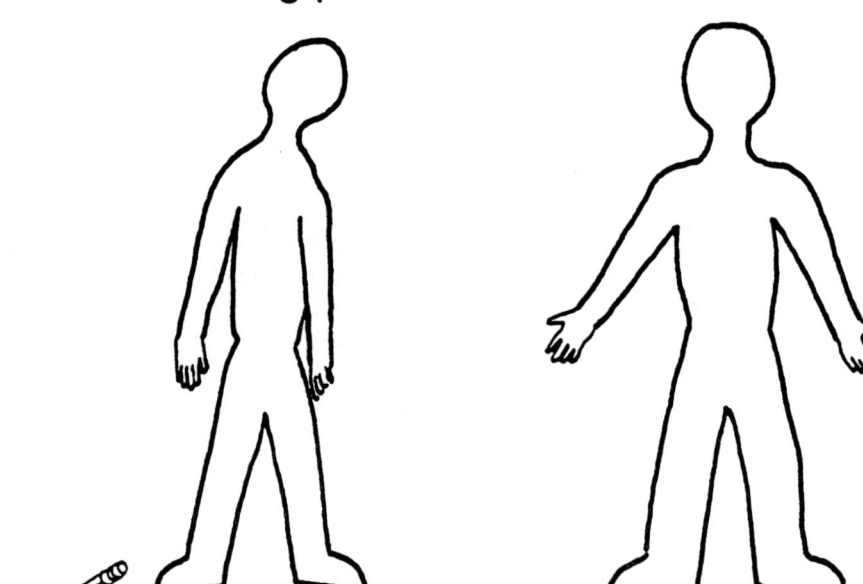

Cross out the one that isn't feeling proud. Now draw your face on the proud person. Can you think of times you have felt proud?

Each of us is special in our own way? In what way are you special?

Hidden Word Game

What would you probably be feeling if...

- you finished all your chores
- you tried your best at your school work
- you played games with good sportmanship
- you were a good friend to others?

Color in all the spaces without dots to find the answer.

"Feeling Lonely" Crossword Puzzle

Complete this crossword puzzle with words that would finish the sentence...

"I feel lonely more often _____."

Down

1. at __ __ __ __ __ __

Across

2. at __ __ __ __

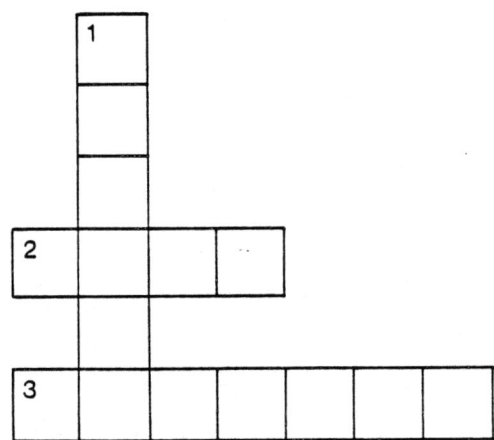

3. while 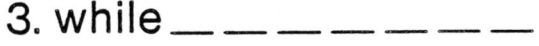 __ __ __ __ __ __ __ __ __

"Feeling Lonely" Letter Association

Write down a word that has something to do with "lonely" for each of the six letters in the word lonely.

L _____

O _____

N _____

E _____

L _____

Y _____

Circle the word that describes how often you feel lonely.

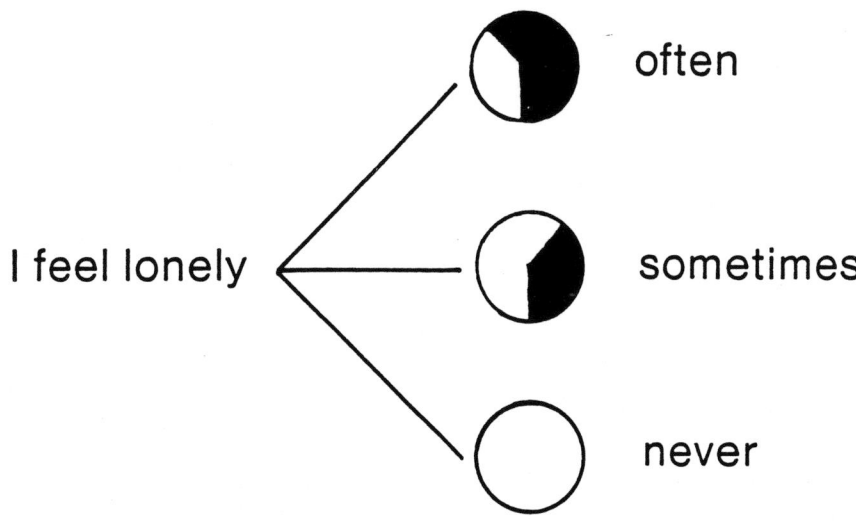

I feel lonely

often

sometimes

never

"Feeling Excited" Multiple Choice

Check the pictures that describe what you do when you feel excited. Then color the ones you have checked.

☐
run and jump

☐
smile

☐
talk loud

☐
hug & kiss

☐
other

"Feeling Excited" Story Completion

You are the writer and director of a play. Describe a scene in the play that would be about you feeling very excited.

SCRIPT

Place: _____

People Present: _____

_____

Activity: _____

_____

Day: _____

Length of time: _____

What you would say: _____

_____

How excited would you be? _____

"Feeling Frustrated" Sentence Completion

Check the box that best finishes the following sentence...

"Someone can help me get rid of my frustration by...

☐ Hugging me

☐ Leaving me alone

☐ Doing something for me

☐ Talking with me

I feel frustrated most often when _____.

"Feeling Frustrated" Secret Code

Use the code below to spell out this important message.

1	2	3	4	5	6	7	8	9	10	11	12	13	14	15	16	17	18	19	20	21	22	23	24	25	26
A	B	C	D	E	F	G	H	I	J	K	L	M	N	O	P	Q	R	S	T	U	V	W	X	Y	Z

"9   3•1•14   20•5•12•12   20•8•1•20

—   — — —   — — — —   — — — —

9   6•5•5•12   6•18•21•19•20•18•1•20•5•4

—   — — — —   — — — — — — — — — —

23•8•5•14   9   3•18•25,   11•9•3•11

— — — —   —   — — —   — — — —

19•15•13•5•20•8•9•14•7,   15•18

— — — — — — — — —   — —

3•18•21•13•16•12•5   21•16   13•25

— — — — — — —   — —   — —

23•15•18•11."

— — — —

"I feel frustrated most often when _____."

"Feeling Smart" Matching

Draw a line to connect the school subjects that are the same.

"Here is my name in my best handwriting."

_____

- -

_____

"Feeling Smart" Completion

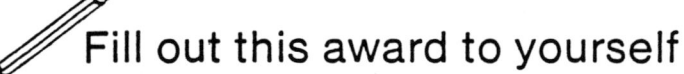 Fill out this award to yourself

This award is given to _____

for being smart in _____.

The way he/she has shown this great

ability is _____

_____

_____

_____

"Someday I hope to do well in _____."

"Feeling Bored" Picture Completion

This space creature is feeling bored today. "I have nothing to do," he says. Show him how to make himself happy. Draw a line connecting him to some games he could play. Can you think of some other things for him to do?

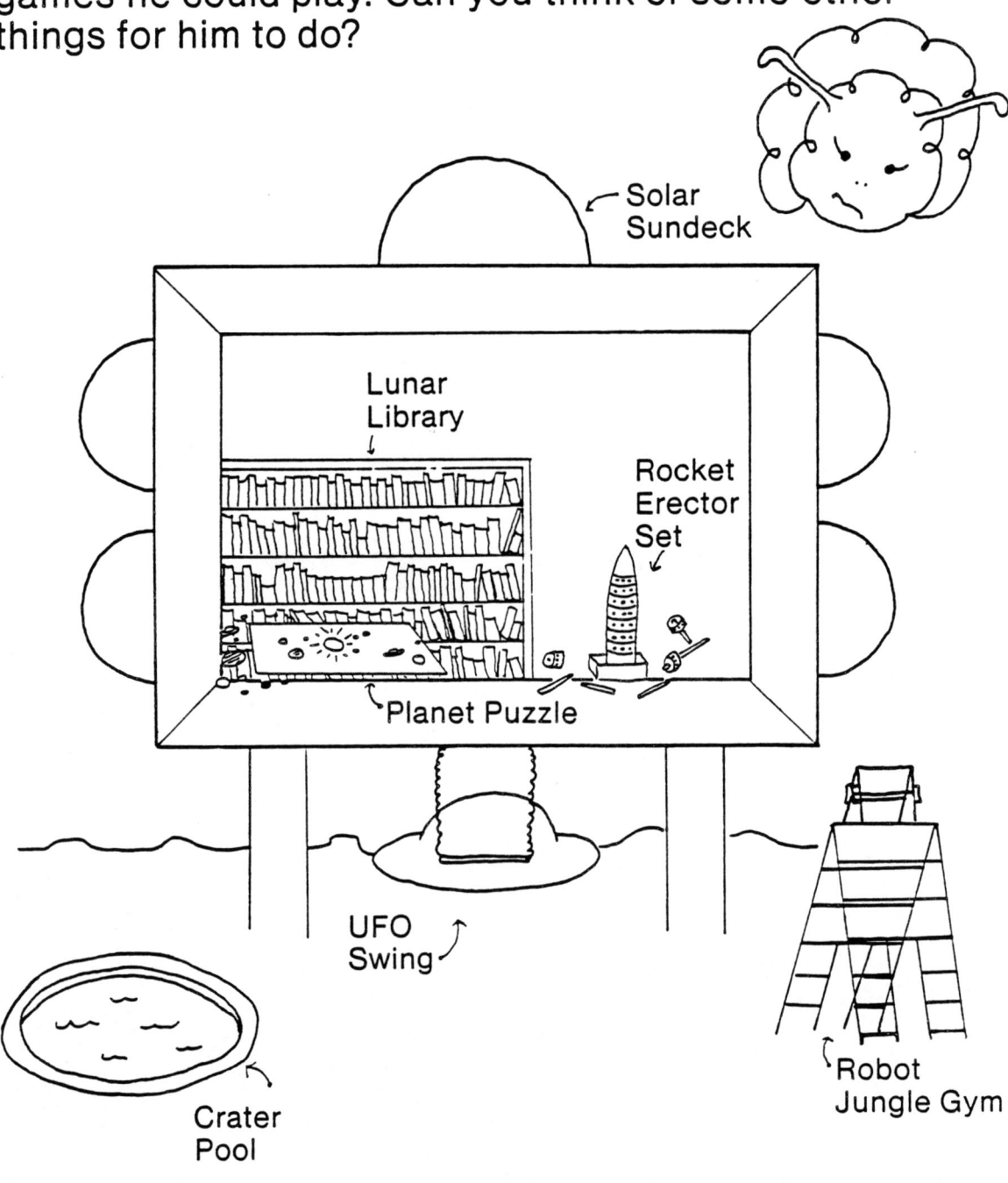

Solar Sundeck

Lunar Library

Rocket Erector Set

Planet Puzzle

UFO Swing

Crater Pool

Robot Jungle Gym

"My Bored Feelings"

Check the one that completes the sentence best for you.

1. "I feel bored...
   - ☐ Alot
   - ☐ Sometimes
   - ☐ Never."

2. "When I feel bored I usually...
   - ☐ Find something to do.
   - ☐ Get into trouble.
   - ☐ Other _____."

3. "When I am bored I usually begin to feel...
   - ☐ Sad
   - ☐ Angry
   - ☐ Lonely."

4. "When I feel bored it is probably because...
   - ☐ I'm not looking for things to do.
   - ☐ I haven't realized it's O.K. to be alone.
   - ☐ I'm not taking responsibility for myself.
   - ☐ Other _____."

"Being Tired" Picture Completion

You can tell that these robots are tired because they (1) are yawning (2) are being grouchy (3) are not functioning well (4) are falling asleep. Complete the drawings with each robot doing one of these things.

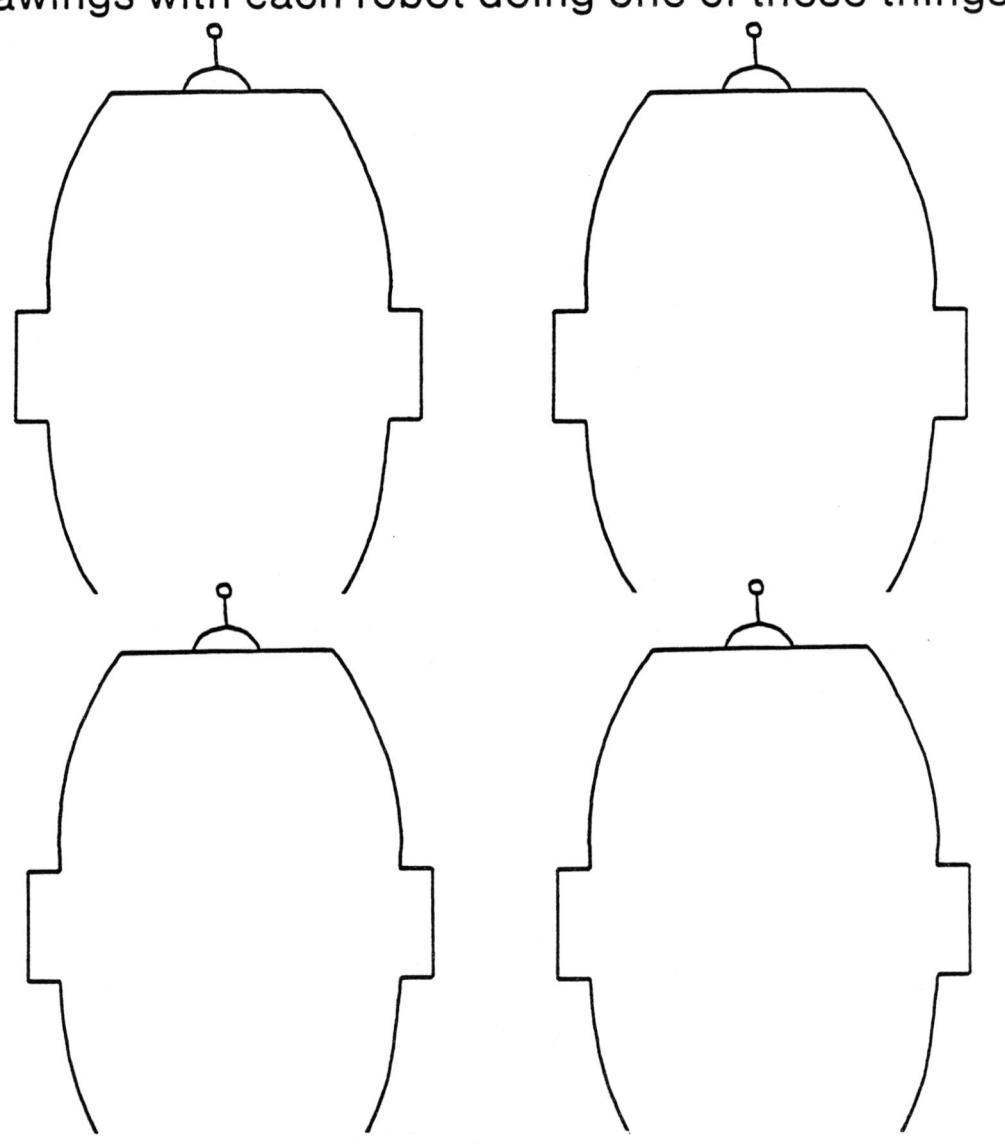

IMPORTANT MESSAGE:
Sometimes when we are tired, things seem worse than they really are.

"Being Tired" Opposites Game

Draw a line between the words that are opposites. All these words have to do with times when we are tired.

early	awake
bedtime	night
crabby	home
play	participate
asleep	often
morning	morning time
watch	alone
school	late
never	nice
together	work

Now circle the words that describe times when you are tired.

"My Feelings at Home"

Draw a line from the pictures below to where they belong in this "At Home" Feelings Chart.

When I get home from school I feel...

When I bring my friends over I feel...

When there is a fight at my house I feel.

When there are problems at my house I feel

Happy

Sad

Excited

Angry

Afraid

Other

"At Home" Feelings Chart

Draw in a face for each of your family members that shows how they usually feel at home. Add faces as you need them. Write the feeling below each picture.

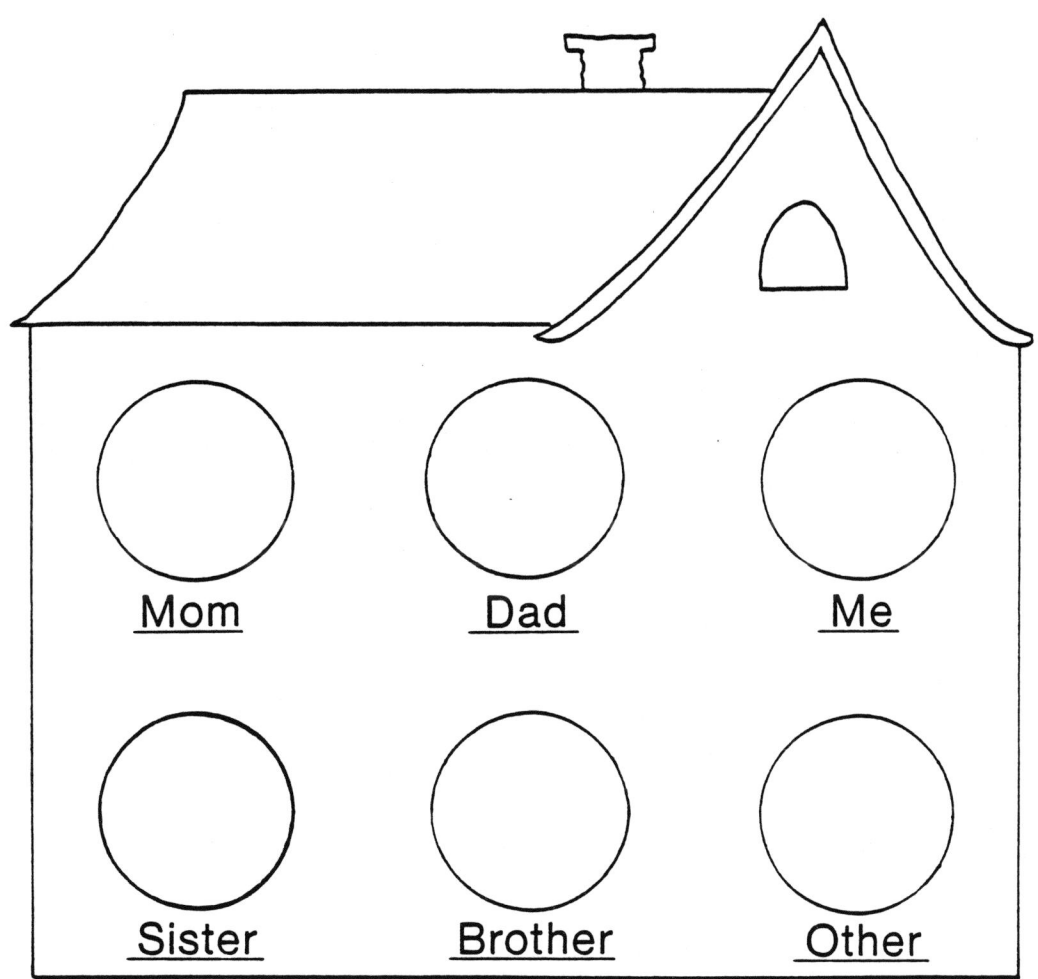

Mom

Dad

Me

Sister

Brother

Other

"My Feelings With Mom and Dad"

Draw a line from the pictures below to where they belong in this "Mom and Dad" Feelings Chart.

When I disobey my parents I feel..

When I hear them say something nice about me I feel..

When my Mom or Dad is very sick I feel..

When they are upset with me I feel..

happy   sad   excited

angry   afraid   other

"My Feelings With Mom and Dad"

Find your way through this maze of feelings. Be careful. The arrows may be misleading. At the end you will find a message about our feelings towards our parents.

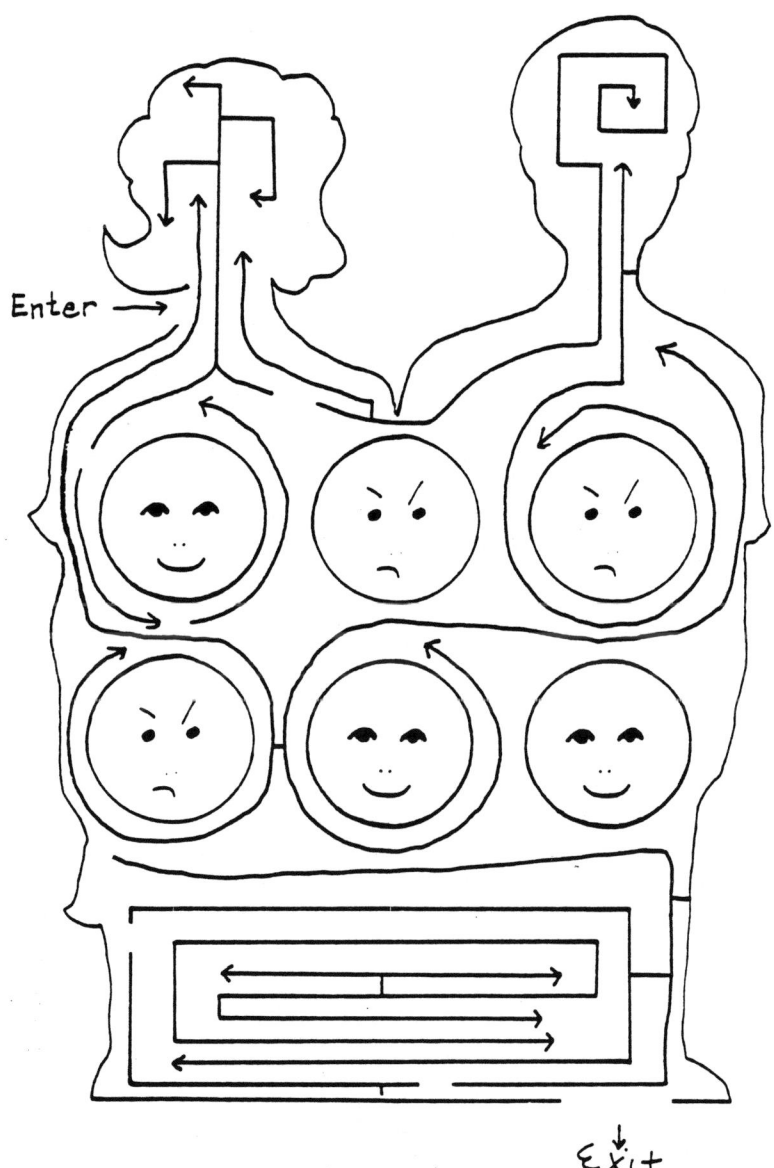

Enter →

Exit

Everybody feels both love and anger towards their parents at different times.
How about you?

"My Feelings With Friends"

Draw a line from the pictures below to where they belong in this Friends Feeling Chart.

When I first meet a new kid I feel...

When the other kids laugh at me I feel...

When no one wants to play with me I feel...

When I get into a fight with my friend I feel...

happy   sad   excited

angry   afraid   other

Coded Message

 This is a coded message about our feelings with friends. To find the missing words, cross out all the letters in each box that appear twice. The remaining letters spell a word. Write the decoded words in the blanks provided.

(1)

Q	O	A	X	P	Q	T	J	U
M	B	L	O	E	B	R	S	U
P	V	X	I	L	V	J	A	R

(2)

S	V	B	A	Q	N	R	N	S	Z	U
B	J	L	P	O	T	Z	S	R	T	K
E	P	U	M	J	A	Q	I	V	M	O

Everyone has _____ when it seems that no one _____ them.

How about you?

109

"My Feelings at School"

Draw a line from the pictures below to where they belong in this "At School" Feelings Chart.

When I get to school I feel...

When it seems like my teacher is being unfair I feel...

When I cannot do my work I feel...

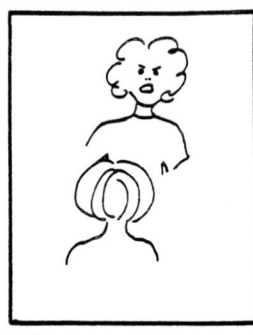

When my teacher yells at me I feel...

"My Feelings at School"

Below is a list of different feelings. Write down a time when you remember feeling each of these emotions at school.

happy _____

sad _____

angry _____

afraid _____

proud _____

embarrassed _____

tired _____

excited _____

Hidden Word Game

 Color in all the spaces without dots to find the missing word in this sentence.

No one is liked by _____.

What is more important, being popular or liking yourself?

Code Game

Use the code below to spell out this important message.

1	2	3	4	5	6	7	8	9	10	11	12	13	14	15	16	17	18	19	20	21	22	23	24	25	26
A	B	C	D	E	F	G	H	I	J	K	L	M	N	O	P	Q	R	S	T	U	V	W	X	Y	Z

14•15•15•14•5   3•1•14   3•15•14•20•18•15•12

___ ___ ___ ___ ___   ___ ___ ___   ___ ___ ___ ___ ___ ___ ___

23•8•1•20   20•8•5•25   6•5•5•12.

___ ___ ___ ___   ___ ___ ___ ___   ___ ___ ___ ___

5•22•5•18•25•15•14•5   3•1•14   4•5•3•9•4•5

___ ___ ___ ___ ___ ___ ___ ___ ___   ___ ___ ___   ___ ___ ___ ___ ___ ___

8•15•23   20•8•5•25   1•18•5   7•15•9•14•7

___ ___ ___   ___ ___ ___ ___   ___ ___ ___   ___ ___ ___ ___ ___

20•15   18•5•19•16•15•14•4   20•15

___ ___   ___ ___ ___ ___ ___ ___ ___   ___ ___

20•8•5•9•18   6•5•5•12•9•14•7•19.

___ ___ ___ ___ ___   ___ ___ ___ ___ ___ ___ ___ ___

happy

sad

angry

proud

hurt

Can you think of some examples?

113

CHAPTER FIVE

ACTIVITIES RELATED TO FAMILY

ACTIVITIES related to family life can be found in this chapter. Clients that may benefit from these therapeutic games include children who are abused, neglected, rejected, or who have strained relations with their parents or siblings due to divorce or other stress. Therapists will find that issues related to family are best addressed in individual therapy. Children usually need the privacy of that setting to open up about this very sensitive part of their lives.

A list of the themes addressed by the activities in this chapter can be found in Table IX, Themes for Activities Related to Family. This table can serve as a guide for readers who need to determine an appropriate intervention for children addressing family problems in therapy. These activities should be used in the middle phase of therapy.

TABLE IX

THEMES FOR ACTIVITIES RELATED TO FAMILY

PAGE	ACTIVITY	THEME
118	"People at My House" Completion	Identifying common interactions among family members
119	"My Family Photography" Completion	Identifying child's perception of his/her family
120	Mom and Dad Completion	Eliciting further disclosure on child's relationship with parents
121	Mom and Dad Word Scramble	
122	Brother and Sister Photograph Completion	Exploring child's relationship with siblings
123	Brother and Sister Opposites	
124	"My Relatives"	Identifying child's extended family situation
125	"My Relatives" Fill-in	Child's perception and relationship with relatives
126	Family Opposites Game	Identifying feelings experienced with family
127	Family Word Search	
128	Multiple Choice	Child reflecting on ways to be a good family member
129	Word Puzzle	
130	Word Completion	Identifying family times together
131	Word Scramble	
132	Picture Completion	Sources of sad feelings with family
133	Opposites Game	
134	"My Special Days"	Child identifying special days with family
135	"Special Times" Fill-in	

TABLE IX *(continued)*

THEMES FOR ACTIVITIES RELATED TO FAMILY

PAGE	ACTIVITY	THEME
136	Word Completion	Identifying ways a child has a bad day with his/her family
137	Bad Days Multiple Choice	
138	"Family Times Together Picture Completion	Child reflecting on how family times could be better
139	"Family Time Together" Completion	
140	"Special Things About My Family" Completion	Child identifying special things about his/her family
141	Word Find	
142	Saying Goodbye Chart	Exploring feelings related to saying goodbye to family
143	Word Completion	

"People at My House" Completion

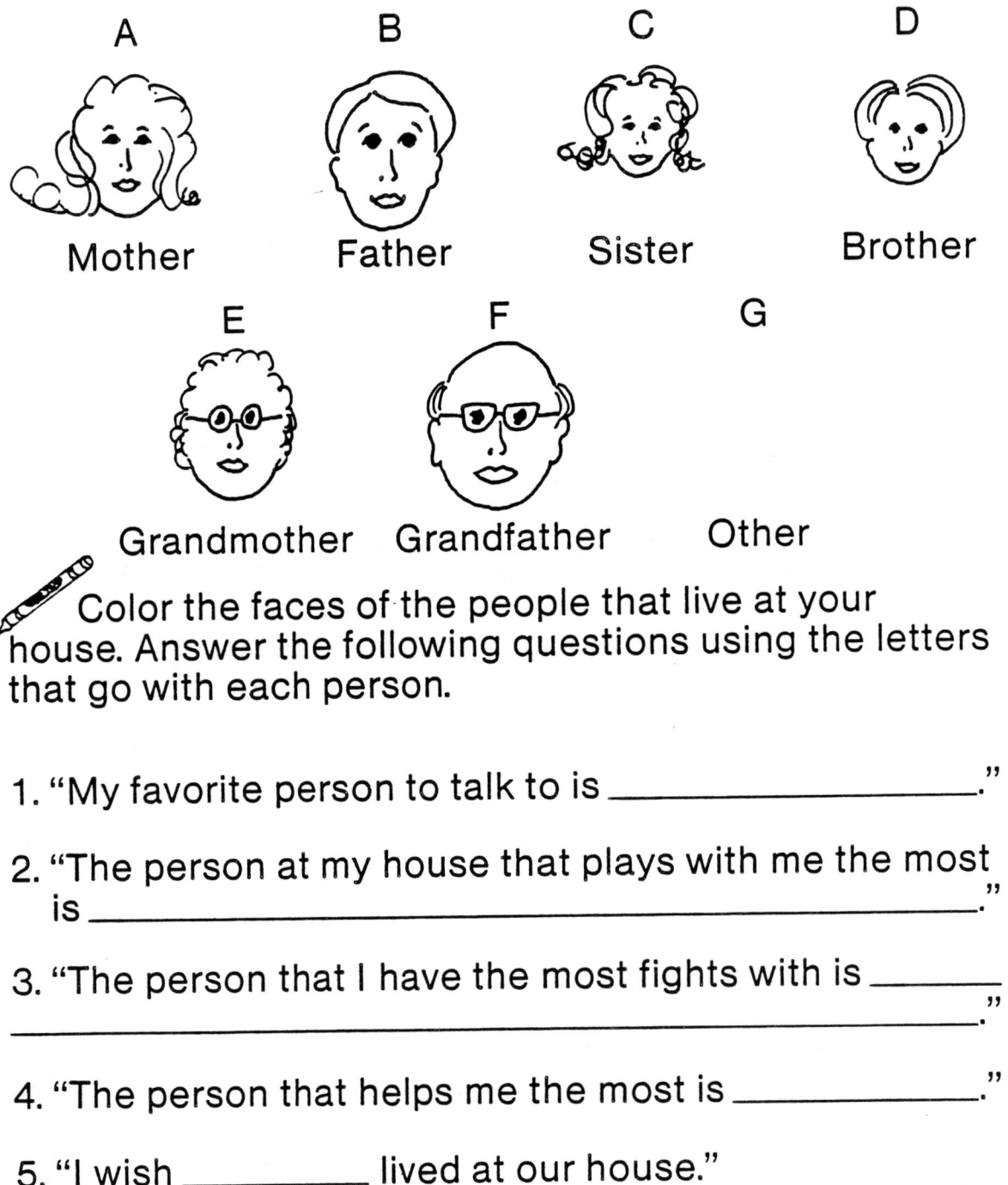

A — Mother
B — Father
C — Sister
D — Brother
E — Grandmother
F — Grandfather
G — Other

Color the faces of the people that live at your house. Answer the following questions using the letters that go with each person.

1. "My favorite person to talk to is _____."

2. "The person at my house that plays with me the most is _____."

3. "The person that I have the most fights with is _____ _____."

4. "The person that helps me the most is _____."

5. "I wish _____ lived at our house."

"My Family Photograph" Completion

✏️ "Here is a photograph of my family sitting in our living room at home."

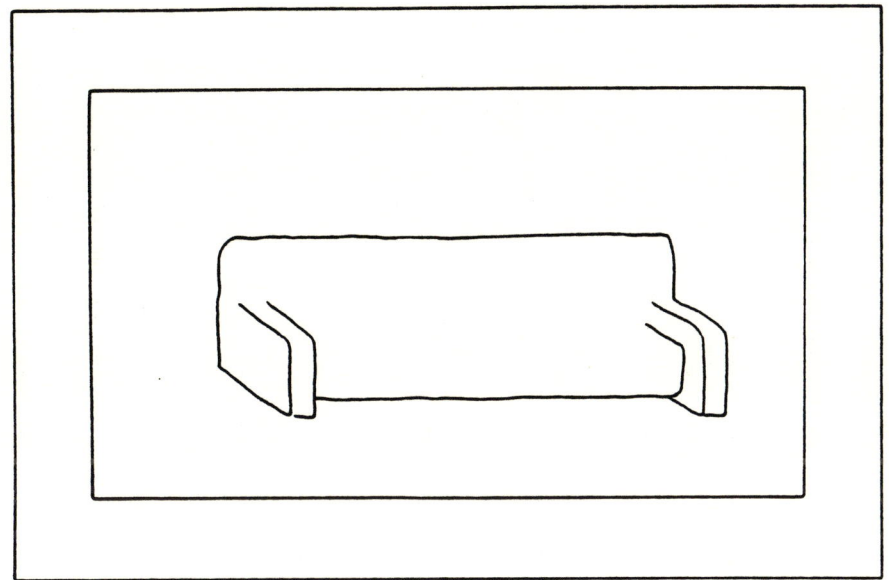

✏️ Circle in blue the family member you get along with the best. Circle in red the family member you have the most problems with.

119

Mom and Dad Completion

Mom   Dad

Pretend this is your Mom and Dad

1. Put a circle around both of them if you live with them both. Put a circle around one of them if you live with only one.

2. Color the one you see & talk with the most yellow.

3. Put an X over the head of the one who punishes you the most.

4. Draw a line under the parent that you think is the most like you.

5. What is one thing you wish your Mom and Dad would do? _____.

Mom and Dad Word Scramble

Dad

Mom

Unscramble the following words to complete the sentences. Then circle the word that answers the sentence for you.

1. "My Mom and Dad are…

    maedrri _____

    paratdese _____

    diorvcde _____."

2. "Most of the time I talk to…

    omm _____

    add _____

    thoer _____."

3. "My Mom and Dad are usually…

    gfithing _____

    firndse _____."

4. "Sometimes I think I am just like my _____."

Brother and Sister
Photograph Completion

Finish this photograph of your family with the number of brothers & sisters you wish you had. Be sure to show which position you would like to have in the family (i.e. youngest, oldest, etc.).

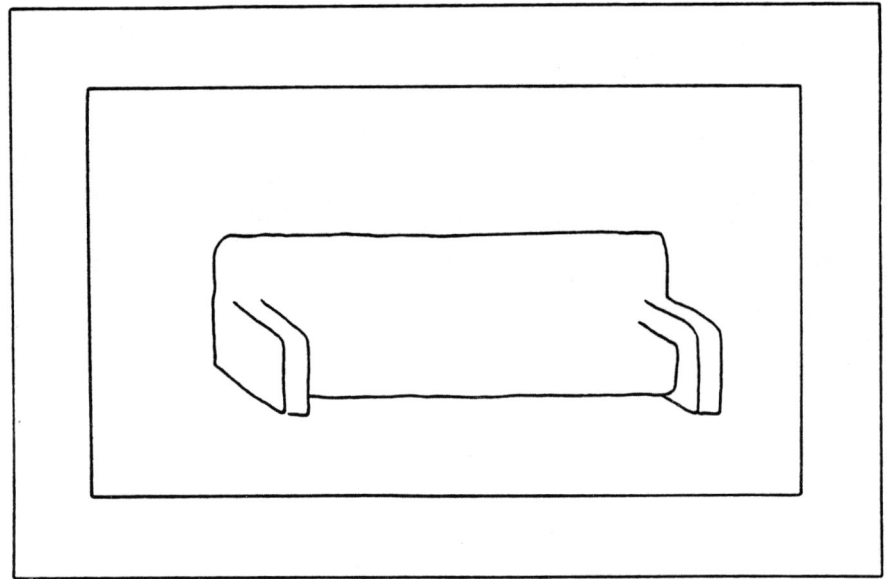

Do you usually get along with your brothers & sisters? ☐ Yes
☐ Sometimes
☐ No

Brother and Sister Opposites

Draw a line between the word in each sentence that is underlined and its opposite in the column of words on the right. Circle the words that apply to you.

1. "Sometimes I want <u>more</u> brothers and sisters."

youngest

2. "Sometimes I want to be the <u>oldest</u>."

no

3. "I would like to have <u>many</u> brothers and sisters."

poorly

4. "I get along <u>well</u> with my brothers and sisters."

less

5. "I <u>have</u> a favorite sibling."

do not have

"My Relatives"

Fill in the branches of this tree with the names of all your relatives. Include aunts, uncles, cousins, & grandparents. Draw in more branches if you need to.

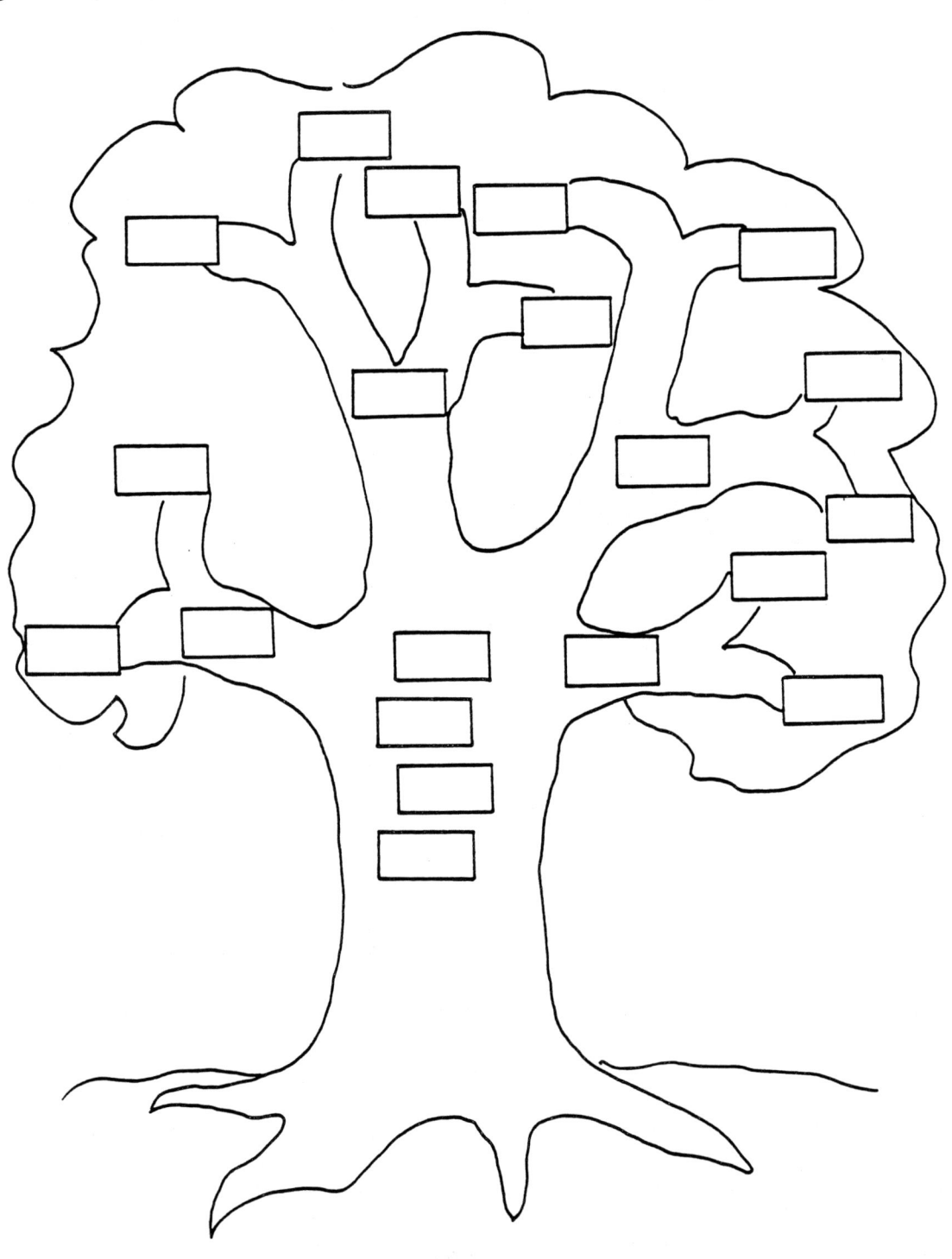

"My Relatives" Fill In

Write down as many words as you can that describe your relatives. These words should begin with the letters in the word "relatives."

R _____

E _____

L _____

A _____

T _____

I _____

V _____

E _____

S _____

Family Opposites Games

Draw a line between the words that are opposites.
All these words have to do with ways a family can feel.

happy   nice

terrible   sad

mean   lonely

friendly   wonderful

great   awful

Name two things you are proud of about your family

_____

_____

Family Word Search

Circle the following words in this word search: great, happy, sad, angry, terrible, good, O.K., nice. All these words have to do with ways a family can feel.

```
m o g r e a t e n o
o k o f e r e r i a
p a o t e m r o c e
s a d p a t r s e r
m o n i o u i n g p
t h a p p y b a f e
r a t s i e l t e s
o a n g r y e y o y
```

Name two things you are proud of about your family

_____

_____

Multiple Choice

This extraterrestrial creature is moving in with an earthling family and has to learn how to get along with them. Draw a line connecting him to the ways he could be a good family member.

Word Puzzle

Write the words that complete the phrases in the puzzle spaces below. The clues have to do with ways you can be a better family member.

Clues

1. Help around the house by doing _____.
2. _____, rather than fight, with brothers and sisters.
3. To work together and help each other is to _____.
4. Go to bed on time and go to _____.
5. _____ to what your parents say and do what they ask.
6. Keep the noise down; when parents ask, be _____.
7. Clean up the place where you sleep; your _____.

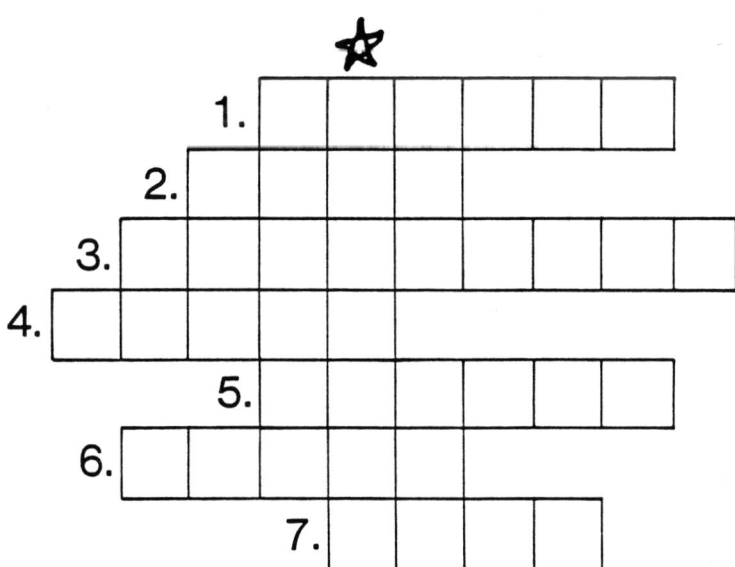

How would you feel if you did all these things at home? Read the word that is formed by the letters under the star.

Word Completion

Finish spelling the following words that all have to do with family time together.

D_ _ nner Ti_ _

Reading a st_ _ _ _

Going on a
t_ _ _

R_ _ _ _ _ bicycles
together

Word Scramble

Unscramble the following words that all have to do with family time together.

1. acvatoin _____

2. nnidre _____

3. eiovms _____

4. klatign _____

5. nasck-time _____

6. VT _____

7. ndekeews _____

8. spotrs _____

Picture Completion

 This space creature is having a sad time with his family. Write a few words or draw a picture about why you think he is sad.

What could he do about this sadness?

Opposites Game

Draw a line between the words that are opposites. All of these words have to do with sad times for families. Circle the words that apply to you.

often	alone
sick	poor
stay	dad
married	dead
mom	brother
hug	talking
rich	play
alive	hit
sister	leave
yelling	divorced
work	never
together	healthy

"My Special Days"

Draw a picture of the most special day at your house. Be sure to include the things you like the best about that day (food, gifts, games, etc.)

"On this special day I feel _____."

"Special Times" Fill-In

✏️ Give a message to your family on this computer by programming in the best way you can spend time together.

Here is the most special way my family can be together...

_____

Day of Week _____

Time of Day _____

Family Members Present _____

Activity _____

This time should be planned into our schedule _____

_____

Word Completion

The following words have to do with things this child may have done that caused him to have a bad day with his family. See if you can finish spelling them.

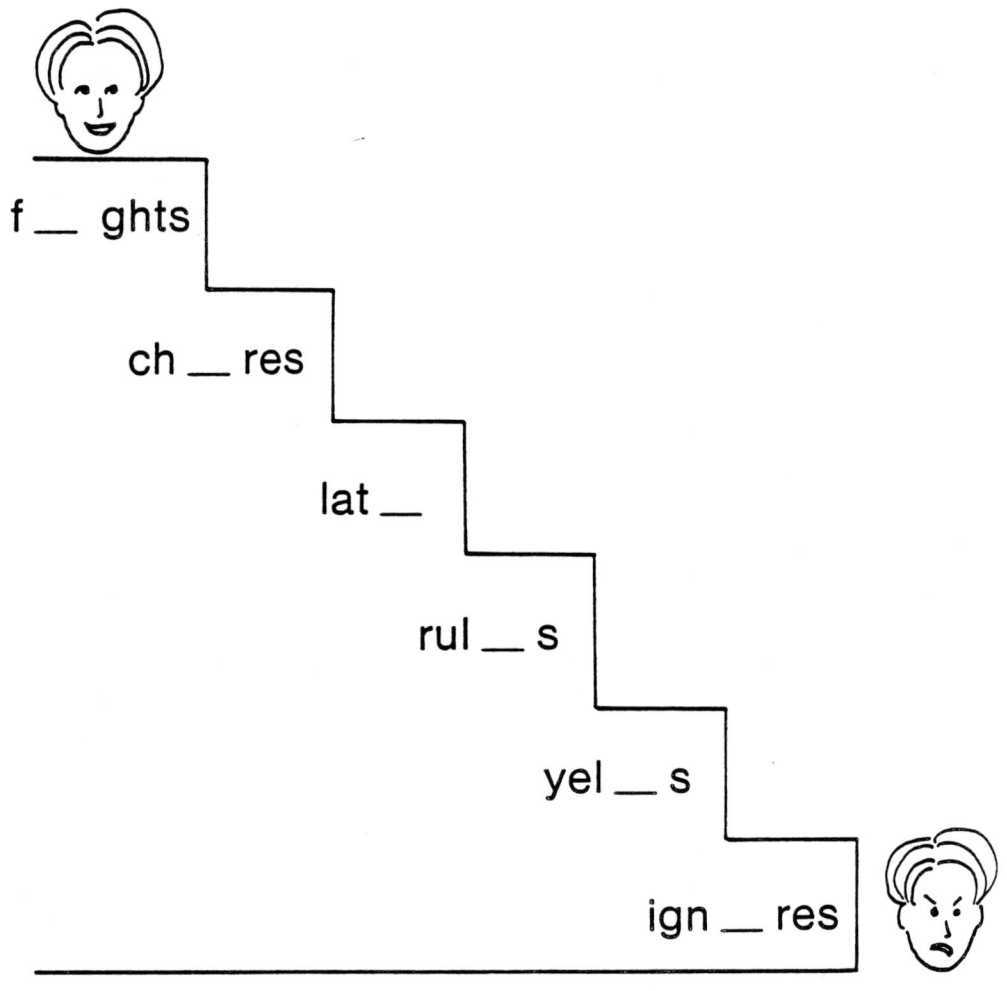

f __ ghts

ch __ res

lat __

rul __ s

yel __ s

ign __ res

Circle the ones that apply to you.

How can you have fewer bad days at home?

Bad Days Multiple Choice

The following circles are situations that may lead to having a bad day with your family. Draw a line under the things you do most often. Put an X on the things you hardly ever do.

do not do chores

do not listen to parents

do not come home on time

do your work too slowly

yell instead of talk

do not follow house rules

do not do homework

get into fights

How can you have fewer bad days at home?

"Family Times Together"
Picture Completion

A genie has appeared from a magic lantern and given you one wish so that you could make family times together better. Draw what you would wish inside this cloud.

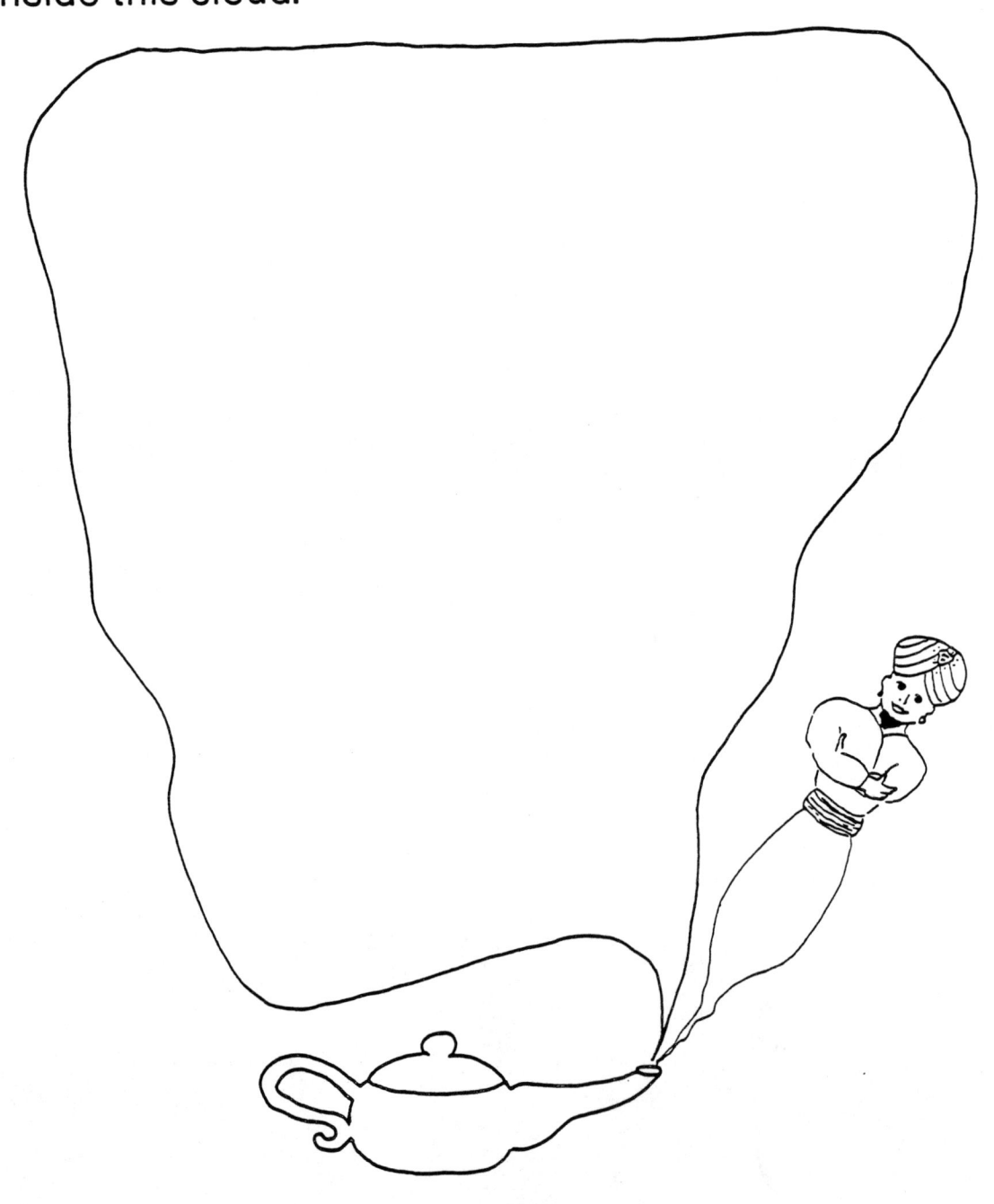

"Family Time Together" Completion

You have been asked to design a program of ways to make your family's times together better.

Family Program

When My Family is together I would like to see

_____

_____

_____

_____

_____

_____

What could you do to make these things happen?

"Special Things About My Family" Completion

 Fill in this award for your family

Special Family Award

My family is special to me because _____

_____

_____

_____

_____

Word Find

Circle the words in this "S" that have to do with Special things about a family. See if you can find all fourteen.

summotedoxeyedihugsefozdir
helpingmucekelgamotu
xeyefzebuditex
sessiksewzugmadarj
readszledritraelmaf
trodsletpmrttunftelaugh
pooflfoodletirnottasmsharing
partiesrigbuinalpminoplaying
snoppanordgniklatmaxsotag
summersnottamsharingsattonriro
vacationsminoplaying
atosxamtalkingrodano
gtammeveningscatnot

Saying Goodbye Chart

Circle the face or faces that show how you would feel if you had to say goodbye to someone in your family.

| O.K. | Sad | Lonely |
| Angry | Afraid | Hurt |

The person in my family that I would miss the most is _____.

Word Completion

Fill in the missing letters to complete the words. These words all have to do with saying goodbye to your family.

1. vis__ __

2. cr __ ing

3. an __ __ y

4. bra __ __

5. sca __ __ d

6. lo __ t

7. h __ g

8. afr __ __ d

9. forgi __ e

10. wr __ __ e

11. lon __ __ y

12. s __ d

The person in my family that I would miss the most is

_____.

CHAPTER SIX

ACTIVITIES RELATED TO SOCIAL SKILLS

IN THIS CHAPTER, the reader will find activities related to the area of social skills. The type of clients who typically will benefit from these activities include youngsters who have no friends, fight often with peers, are teased frequently, have trouble keeping friends, etc. Clinicians working with children in group therapy may find these activities particularly helpful, since one of the primary benefits of that treatment modality is the enhancement of social skills.

These interventions are most appropriate in the treatment process during the middle phase. In Table X, Themes for Activities Related to Social Skills, the reader will find a complete listing of themes addressed by activities in this chapter. Professionals can use this table as a guide when selecting activities and themes related to a child's social skills.

TABLE X

THEMES FOR ACTIVITIES RELATED TO SOCIAL SKILLS

PAGE	ACTIVITY	THEME
148	"Friends for Me" Fill-in	Exploring a child's perception of a good friend
149	"Friends for Me" Completion	
150	"Meeting New Friends" Map	Having child explore ways and places to meet friends
151	Crossword Puzzle	
152	"Friends in My Neighborhood"	Exploring friendships in child's neighborhood
153	"Friends at School" Opposites Game	Exploring child's friendships at school
154	"My Best Friend" Path	Having child disclose about his/her best friend
155	"My Best Friend" Picture Completion	
156	Multiple Choice	Exploring child's fears about making friends
157	Sentence Maze	
158	"Me as a Friend" Multiple Choice	Increasing child's awareness of his/her friendship qualities
159	"Me as a Friend" Completion	
160	"Being a Better Friend" Completion	Child exploring ways to be a better friend
161	"Being a Better Friend" Crossword Puzzle	
162	"Things I Like to Do With Friends" Completion	Having child share things he/she enjoys with friends
163	"Things I Like to Do With Friends" Sentence Completion	
164	"Talking to Friends" Word Search	Exploring the times when a child likes to talk with a friend
165	"Talking to My Friends" Completion	

TABLE X *(continued)*

THEMES FOR ACTIVITIES RELATED TO SOCIAL SKILLS

PAGE	ACTIVITY	THEME
166	"Showing Friends You Like Them" Phrase Completion	Increasing child's awareness of how to show a friend you like him/her
167	"Showing Friends you Like Them" Game	
168	"Helping My Friend" Completion	Child exploring ways to help a friend
169	"Helping My Friend" Opposites	
170	"Asking My Friends for Help"	Exploring ways to ask for help from friends
171	"Asking My Friends for Help" Code Game	
172	Friendship Path	Increasing child's awareness of how to make up with a friend after a fight
173	"Saying I am Sorry to My Friend"	
174	"Keeping My Friends" Fill-in	Exploring child's long term friendships
175	Coded Message	
176	"Thank You Card" Completion	Increasing child's awareness of ways to thank a friend
177	Word Scramble	
178	"Troubles with My Friends"	Exploring problems a child has had with friends
179	Word Scramble Sentence Completion	
180	Friendship Maze	Helping child to identify other qualities to seek in friendships
181	"Friendship Wishes for Me"	
182	"Keeping My Friends for a Long Time" Phrase Completion	Child looking at other ways to keep friendship
183	"Keeping My Friends for a Long Time" Completion	
184	"Saying Goodbye to My Friends"	Exploring the friendships that a child still misses
185	Goodbye Card Completion	

"Friends for Me" Fill-In

Complete this drawing of an ideal friend for you.

Age:

Good at:

Helps me:

We play:

I like the
way he/she:

"Friends for Me" Completion

Complete the sentences below about you and friendships.

1. "A friend to me is _____."

2. "I would like to have _____."

3. "Most of the time I _____ to be with my friends."

4. "Friends are ususally _____ to me."

5. "I usually want to be with my friends when _____
_____."

6. "Most of my friends are
   ☐ older
   ☐ the same age
   ☐ younger."

"Meeting New Friends" Map

 This girl just moved to a new neighborhood and wants to make some friends. Draw a line connecting her to the best places to meet new friends on this neighborhood map. Can you think of any other good places to meet friends?

Home

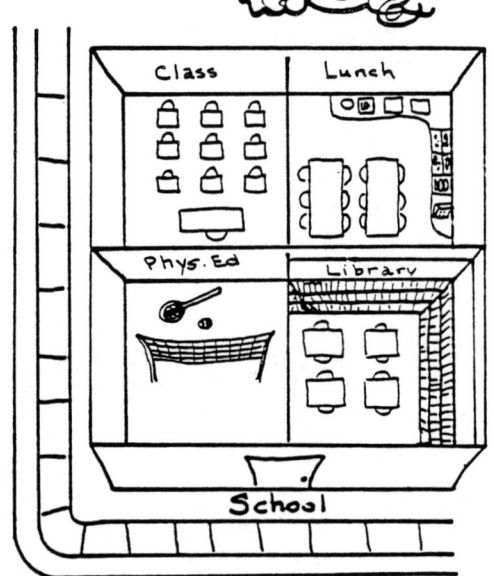

Class   Lunch

Phys. Ed   Library

School

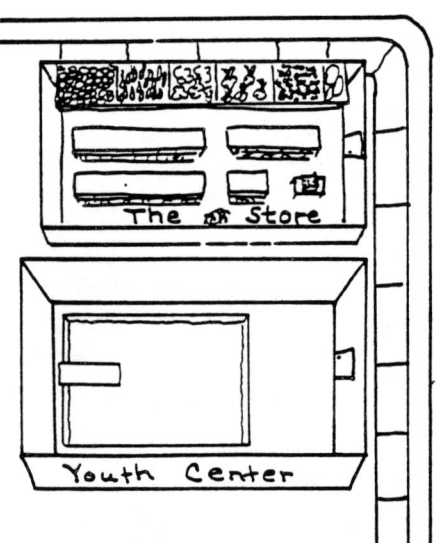

The Store

Youth Center

The Park

Crossword Puzzle

Complete this crossword puzzle. Hint: All the answers have to do with good places to meet new friends.

Down

1. Free play
3. Place to learn math, reading, science, etc.
5. Screen games
7. Midday Meal
9. Activities you play
10. Special interest groups
11. Place you buy things

Across

2. Place teachers & students go
4. Opponents that play baseball, soccer, etc.
6. The area where you live
8. Exercise class

"Friends In My Neighborhood"

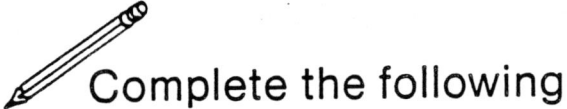 Complete the following

1. "There are alot of kids in my neighborhood."
   - ☐ Yes
   - ☐ No

2. "I have the most friends
   - ☐ at school
   - ☐ at home."

3. "You would have alot of friends in my neighborhood if you could _____ very well."

4. "Most of the time I play with my neighborhood friends...
   - ☐ Very well
   - ☐ O.K.
   - ☐ Not very well."

"Friends at School" Opposites Game

Draw a line between the opposite words that complete this sentence.

"Friends at school can be _____ ."

unpopular	snobby
bright	boys
good	nice
older	sad
girls	fun
friendly	bad
happy	talkative
boring	younger
quiet	dull
mean	popular

153

"My Best Friend" Path

Sometimes it's hard to find a "best" friend. But when you do, it is very special. See if you can find the line that leads you to your best friend.

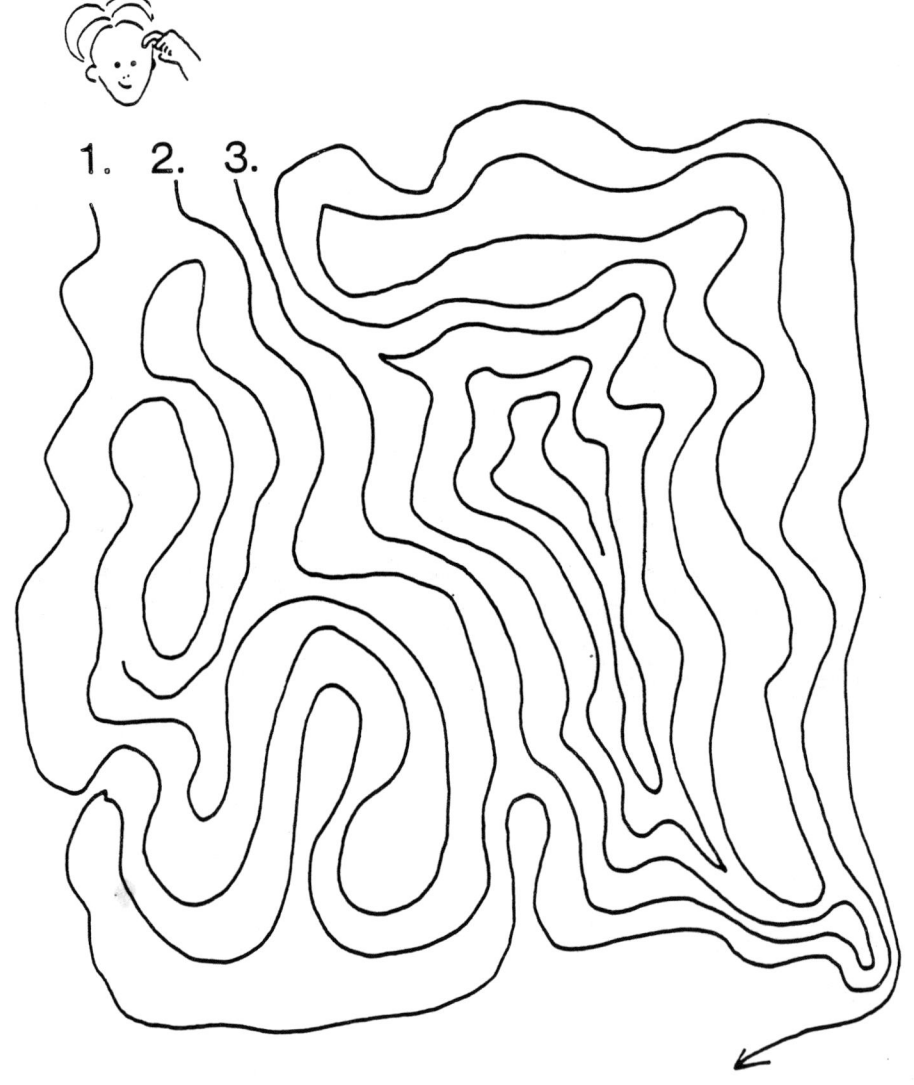

1.   2.   3.

My best friend _____

Age _____

Lives _____

Good at _____

"My Best Friend" Picture Completion

Complete this picture so that it has something to do with you and your best friend.

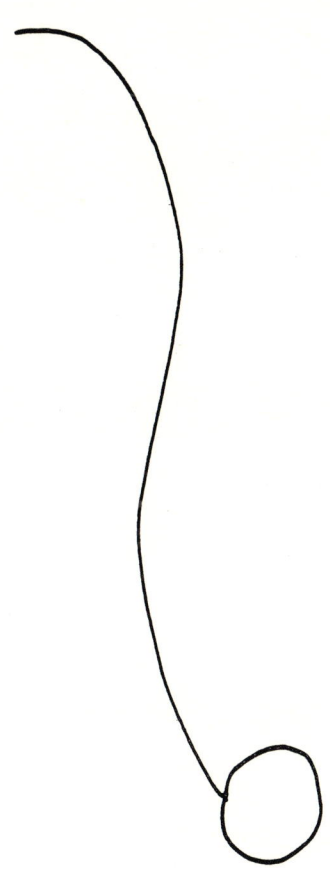

Multiple Choice

Below are some fears that people have sometimes when they think about making new friends. Color the fears that you have had.

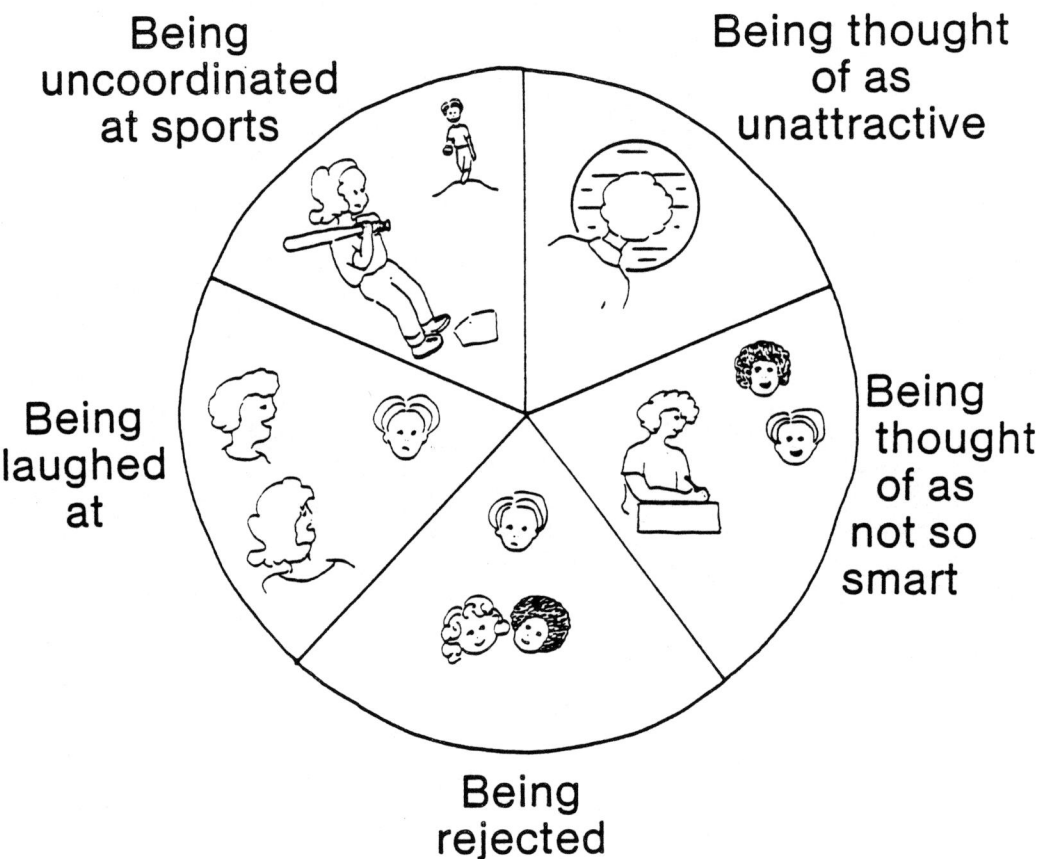

Being uncoordinated at sports

Being thought of as unattractive

Being laughed at

Being thought of as not so smart

Being rejected

What can you do about those fears?

Sentence Maze

Follow the path that spells out a message about making new friends.

What can you do on those days?

"Me as a Friend" Multiple Choice

Circle all the words that describe why other kids like you as a friend.

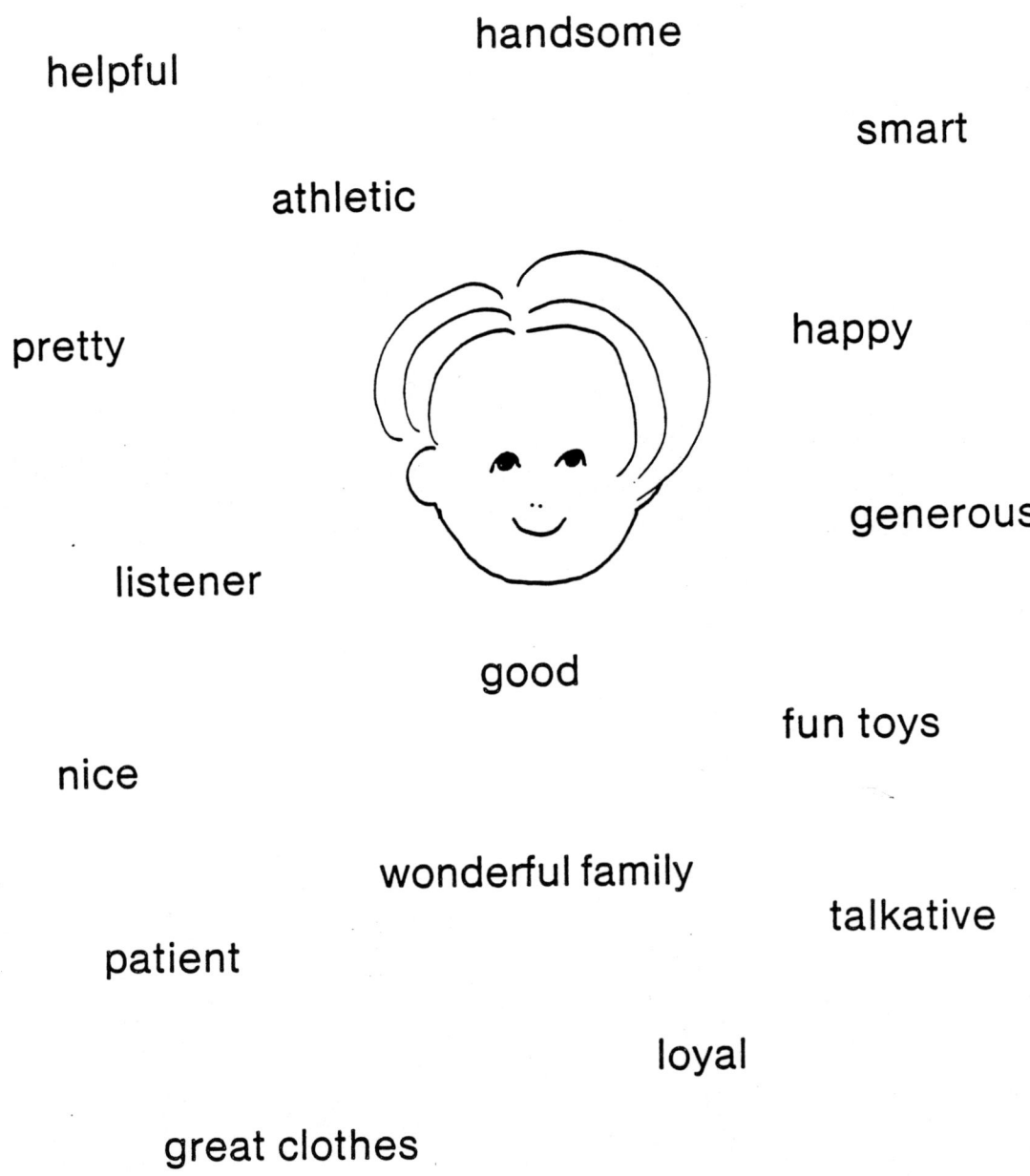

handsome

helpful

smart

athletic

pretty

happy

generous

listener

good

fun toys

nice

wonderful family

talkative

patient

loyal

great clothes

"Me as a Friend" Completion

Pretend you are advertising your friendship. Write or draw on this billboard something about you that will attract friends.

"Being a Better Friend" Completion

 You have just developed a method that will help people to become better friends. Put your commercial for it on T.V.

"Be a Better Friend" Crossword Puzzle

Complete this crossword puzzle with words that have to do with being a better friend.

Across
1. Sticks by someone
3. Give part of or let someone else use
5. Good to friends
7. Participate in games

Down
2. Hear someone
4. Understanding
6. Give a hand
8. Tell your friend something

Circle all the words that apply to ways you could be a better friend.

"Things I like to Do with Friends" Completion

 Show through this window what you and a friend are enjoying together.

"Things I like to Do with Friends" Sentence Completion

Write a sentence about you and a friend doing something that includes the following objects or concepts.

1. playing a sport _____

2. computer _____

3. homework _____

4. bicycle _____

5. building something _____

6. tape recorder _____

7. money _____

8. talking to each other _____

Now circle the activity that you like to do best with your friends. If it is not included, write it here _____

_____.

"Talking to Friend" Word Search

When you have something on your mind it's nice to talk to a friend. See how many times you can find the word "TALK" below and circle them.

```
F T A L K F Y S
T A L K T A L K
E L T A L K R S
M K T F M N T U
T A L K T A L K
```

"Talking to My Friends" Completion

Complete the following:

1. Which feelings do you share with your friends? Circle them below.

happy   sad   angry   proud   hurt

2. Circle the face that shows you how often you talk to your friends.

Alot   Sometimes   Hardly ever

3. Complete the sentences below by circling all the words that apply to you.

"I usually talk to my friends about my...

problems	trips	joys	other."
school work	toys	hobbies	
parents	feelings	clubs	

165

"Showing Friends You Like Them" Phrase Completion

How can you show a friend that you like him or her? Complete these sentences by drawing a line to the correct picture.

1. Giving a...

2. Sharing your...

3. Shaking their...

4. Giving them a hug or...

5. Calling them on the...

6. Asking them to your...

7. Sending a...

8. Saying "I like _____ "...

"Showing Friends You Like Them" Game

Each player uses coins as game markers and dice. Flip a coin to advance. Heads means that you move ahead one space; tails means two spaces. Before each player moves the marker, they must think of a different way to show a friend that they like them. If they forget to share that information they lose a turn. The first player to reach the finish line wins.

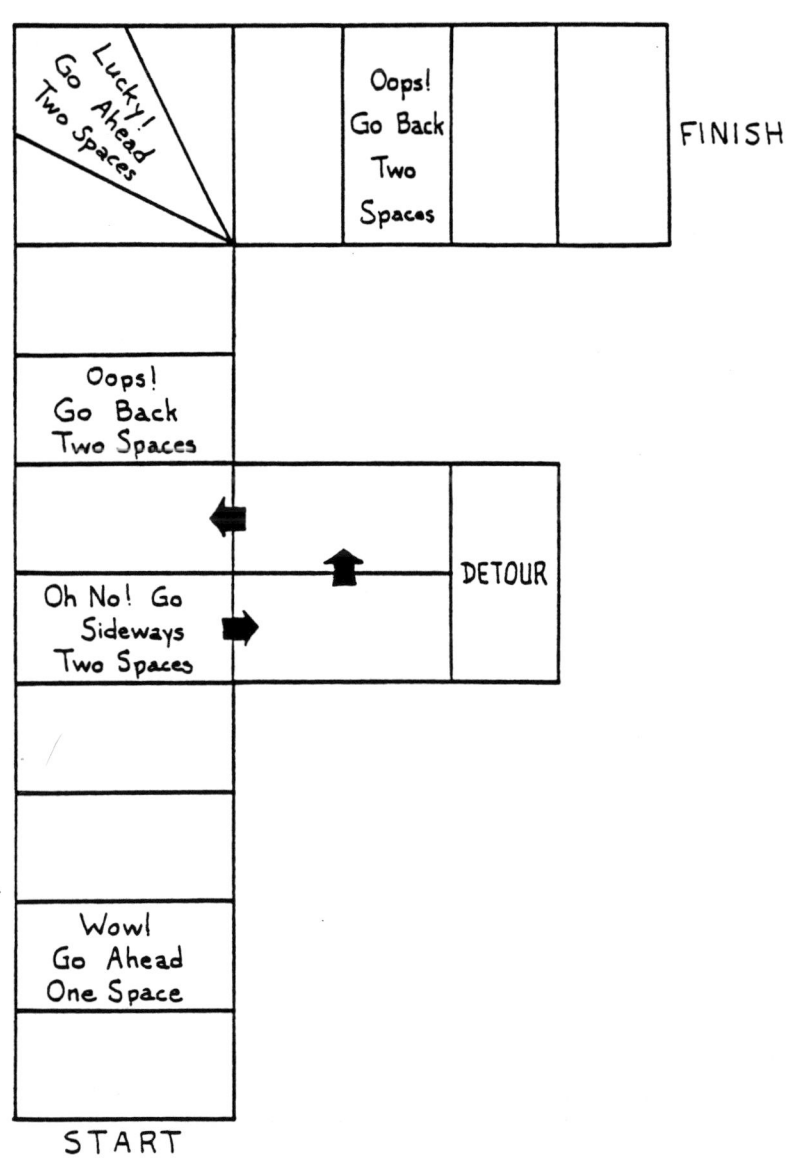

Lucky! Go Ahead Two Spaces

Oops! Go Back Two Spaces

FINISH

Oops! Go Back Two Spaces

DETOUR

Oh No! Go Sideways Two Spaces

Wow! Go Ahead One Space

START

"Helping My Friend" Completion

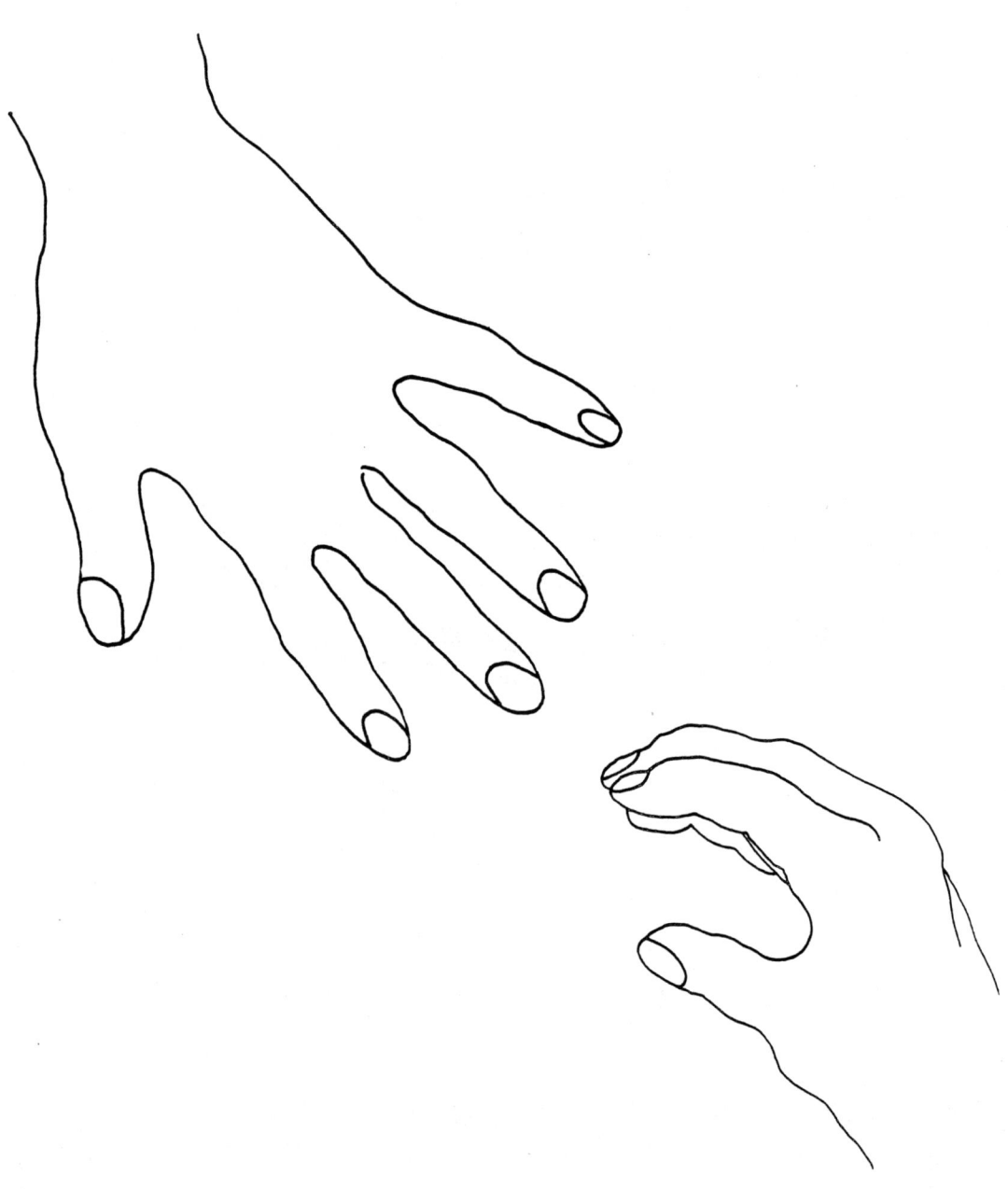 Write on each finger a way you can help out a friend.

"Helping My Friend" Opposites

Draw a line between the words that are opposites.
All of these words have to do with helping a friend.
Then circle the ones that apply to you.

accept	laugh
work	alot
a little	listen
home	sad
talk	give
happy	lonely
receive	teach
learn	dishonest
friendly	play
fight	hug
cry	invite
honest	school

"Asking My Friends For Help"

 Complete the following:

1. "I have asked my friends for help...
   ☐ often   ☐ sometimes   ☐ never."

2. "When I need help from my friend I feel...

   ☐ O.K.   ☐ Embarrassed   ☐ Angry."

3. "I would rather...
   ☐ ask a friend to help
   ☐ do the task myself."

4. "The one friend who I can always count on is

   _____."

"Asking My Friends for Help" Code Game

The following is a message about asking friends for help. Use the number code below to figure out this message.

1	2	3	4	5	6	7	8	9	10	11	12	13	14	15	16	17	18	19	20	21	22	23	24	25	26
A	B	C	D	E	F	G	H	I	J	K	L	M	N	O	P	Q	R	S	T	U	V	W	X	Y	Z

"9•20   9•19   9•13•16•15•18•20•1•14•20

___ ___   ___ ___   ___ ___ ___ ___ ___ ___ ___ ___ ___

6•15•18   1   6•18•9•5•14•4

___ ___ ___   ___   ___ ___ ___ ___ ___ ___

20•15   7•9•22•5   1•14•4

___ ___   ___ ___ ___ ___   ___ ___ ___

18•5•3•5•9•22•5   8•5•12•16."

___ ___ ___ ___ ___ ___ ___   ___ ___ ___ ___

171

Friendship Path

This is a friendship path. It shows ways that friends can get into fights and ways that they can make up again. Fill in the empty blocks with other ways you can think of that friends go through that process.

"Saying I Am Sorry to My Friend"

Complete the following:

1. "I usually know when I hurt my friend
   - ☐ Yes
   - ☐ Sometimes
   - ☐ No."

2. "I hurt my friends alot
   - ☐ Yes
   - ☐ No."

3. "If I hurt one of my friends I usually do this...
   - ☐ Say I am sorry
   - ☐ Give them a gift
   - ☐ Just try to forget about it."

4. "For me to say I am sorry to a friend is...
   - ☐ Hard
   - ☐ Easy."

5. "One friend I would like to say I'm sorry to is

_____ ."

"Keeping My Friends" Fill In

Write the names of all your friends on the petals of this flower. Color your most recent friend blue, your best friend yellow, and the friend you've had for the longest time in red. The petals may have more than one color. Now finish coloring the rest of your plant.

MY FRIENDSHIP PLANT

Coded Message

Fill in the missing words of this message about keeping your friendships. To decode the missing words, cross out all the letters that appear twice among the large letters below. Then write the words in the blanks provided.

(1) L B J E S T I X
G B A O X N J O E

(2) G E M L F T Y
S Y I K E K M L

Make sure you have some (1) _____ friendships.

They are wonderful (2) _____ to give yourself.

Thank You Card Completion

Complete this thank you card to a friend you would like to thank for something. Cut it out, decorate it, and give it to your friend.

Dear_____,

I want to

thank you

for_____

_____

_____

Your friend,

Word Scramble

All these words have to do with saying thank you to a friend. Unscramble them and circle the ones that you would use.

1. gfit _____

2. crda _____

3. hgu _____

4. isks _____

5. clal _____

6. sarhe _____

7. misle _____

8. sahke _____

"Troubles with My Friends"

Draw or write all the troubles you have had with friends in this bag of toubles.

Word Scramble Sentence Completion

Unscramble the words in boxes and write them in the blanks provided. All these sentences are about having troubles with friends.

1. Everyone has |tolesrub| _____ with friends.

2. It is important to talk with your |dernifs| _____ about your troubles.

3. It is O.K. to be |grany| _____ with your friends.

4. When you stay angry with a friend for too long it is more |tculiffdi| _____ to work out your troubles.

5. Often times both friends are at |lutaf| _____ in an an argument.

Friendship Maze

Find your way through this maze to TRUE FRIENDSHIP. You may take a wrong turn just as we all do sometimes when we look for the wrong type of friends for ourselves. Look and see what makes good friendships around us.

True Friendship

Enter Here

"Friendship Wishes for Me"

Make three wishes about you and your friendships. Write them on the list below & circle the one you feel you have the best chance of getting with your own efforts. Then give yourself an assignment that will achieve that wish & write it on the assignment sheet. Cut it off, take it home, & remember to do it.

Three Friendship Wishes

1. _____

2. _____

3. _____

Assignment

I want to work on wish number _____

so I will _____

_____

_____

"Keeping My Friends for a Long Time" Phrase Completion

Connect the phrase with the word that best completes it. Each of these phrases would make a good ending for the sentence, "Keeping friends for a long time means..."

1. playing with them _____   feelings

2. sharing your _____   one another

3. talking with _____   compliments

4. being _____   often

5. giving them _____   care

6. telling them you _____   nice

Now go back and circle the ones that apply to you. Can you add other ways to keep friends? _____

_____

"Keeping My Friends for a Long Time" Completion

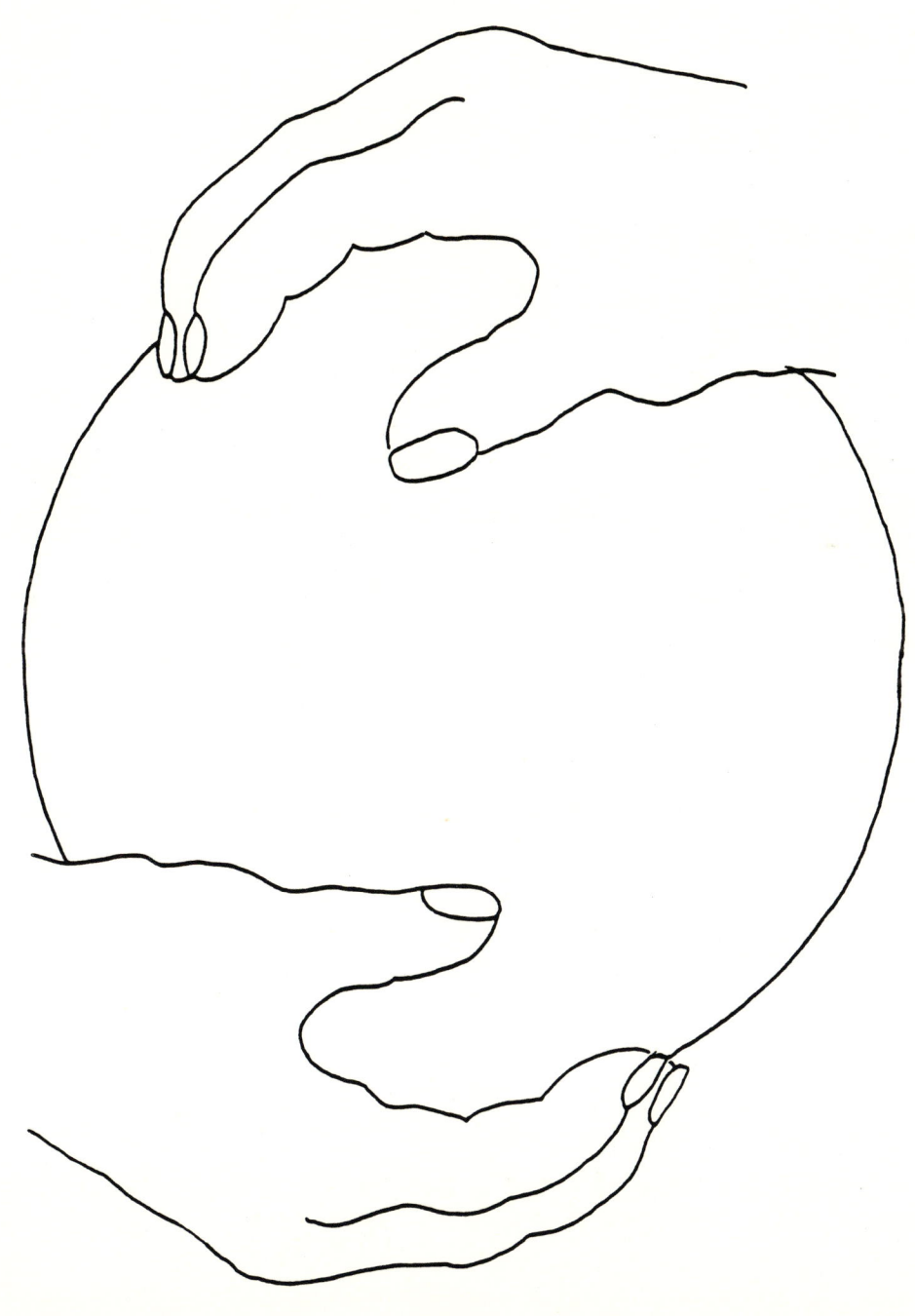 Draw a picture on this ball to show how these two friends will remain friends for a long time.

"Saying Good-Bye to My Friends"

Complete this sentence by writing the names of the friends that you had to say good-bye to in the empty circles.

"I still miss _____

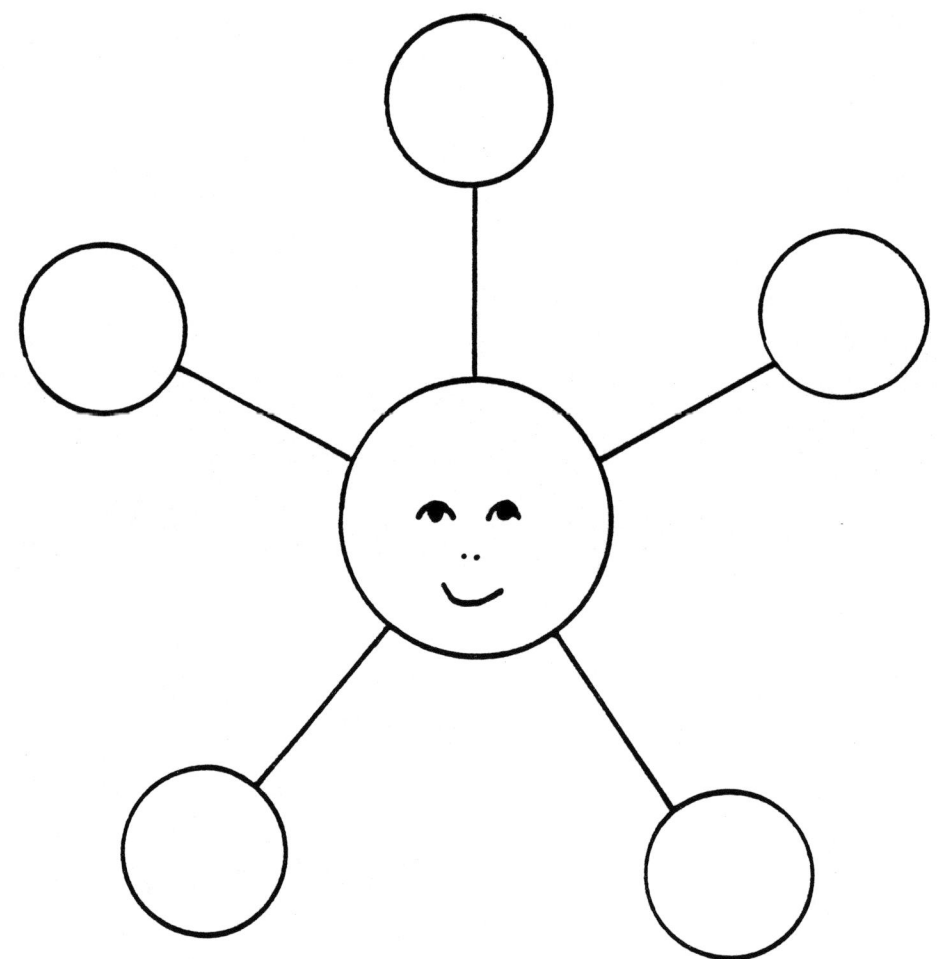

Put a check by the one you miss the most. Put an X by the one you never had a chance to say good-bye to. Draw a line under the ones you still write or talk to.

Goodbye Card Completion

✏️ Cut out and complete this card to a friend that you were not able to say good-bye to.

Goodbye, My Friend	Dear_____, I still miss you because____ _____ _____ Love, _____

185

CHAPTER SEVEN

ACTIVITIES RELATED TO SCHOOL

IN THIS CHAPTER, the reader will find a number of activities related to school. The type of children who would typically benefit from these activities include the learning disabled student, the child functioning below grade level yet having greater potential, the school phobic, the gifted student who is teased by others, etc. Many times, therapists will find that the child referred for counseling has school problems as part of the reason for the need for treatment. Readers are encouraged to stay in contact with a child's teachers during therapy in order to more accurately evaluate progress in this area of treatment.

These interventions are usually more appropriate during the middle phase of therapy when a clinician is able to address a child's problem areas. In Table XI, Themes for Activities Related to School, the reader will find a listing of all themes covered by activities in this chapter. Therapists should use this table as a guide when selecting school-related activities for a child in treatment.

TABLE XI

THEMES FOR ACTIVITIES RELATED TO SCHOOL

PAGE	ACTIVITY	THEME
190 191	"Me at School" Completion Opposites Game	Exploring child's perception of his/her school performance
192 193	Word Jumble Crossword Puzzle	Exploring child's feelings about school
194 195	Number Search "Me and My Classmates" Completion	Having child talk about friends at school
196 197	"Design a Teacher" Cut Out "Me and My Teachers" Completion	Eliciting child's feelings about teachers
198 199	"Me as a Student" Completion Student-O-Meter	Exploring child's perception about self as a student
200 201	Picture Completion Brainstorm Game	Increasing child's awareness of sources of happiness at school
202 203	"Good Days at School" Path Guess What Game	Increasing child's awareness of how to be happier at school
204 205	"Me and My School Work" Sentence Completion Opposites Game	Exploring child's perception about his/her school work
206 207	Reading Fill-in Coded Story	Eliciting child's feelings about reading
208 209	Maze Coded Message	Exploring child's feelings about math

TABLE XI *(continued)*

THEMES FOR ACTIVITIES RELATED TO SCHOOL

PAGE	ACTIVITY	THEME
210	Home from School Picture Completion	Exploring sources of enjoyment after school
211	Home from School Game	
212	Take a Walk through Testland	Having child disclose feelings about tests
213	Report Card Fill-in	Having child identify an ideal report card for self
214	What's Wrong	Exploring ways a child has bad days at school
215	Word Matching Game	
216	"Getting Help" Completion	Exploring child's feelings about asking for help at school
217	Feeling Proud at School	Exploring child's sources of pride at school
218	Saying Goodbye Sentence Completion	Exploring child's feelings about schools and classes
219	Picture Fill-in	

"Me at School" Completion

Complete the following sentences

1. My favorite time at school is

2. Here is a word I can spell

3. Here is some math I can do

4. Here is my name in my best handwriting

- -

5. At school I am this kind of student

☐ Great

☐ O.K.

☐ Not so great

Opposites Game

Draw a line between the words about school that are opposites. Circle the ones that apply to you.

walk	smart
great	print
low	fun
multiply	punished
dumb	sad
work	awful
cursive	end
afraid	play
beginning	ride
praised	divide
happy	high
boring	comfortable

Word Jumble

 Color in the word in this word jumble
that best completes the sentence...
    "If I stopped going to school, I would feel _____."

Why would you feel that way?

Crossword Puzzle

Complete this crossword puzzle. All the words have to do with school & what it might mean to you.

Across

1. Understanding new work
3. Studying a book
5. Athletics
7. Opposite of sad

Down

2. Buddies
4. Adding & Subtracting
6. Feel unhappy
8. Times when you go off school grounds with class

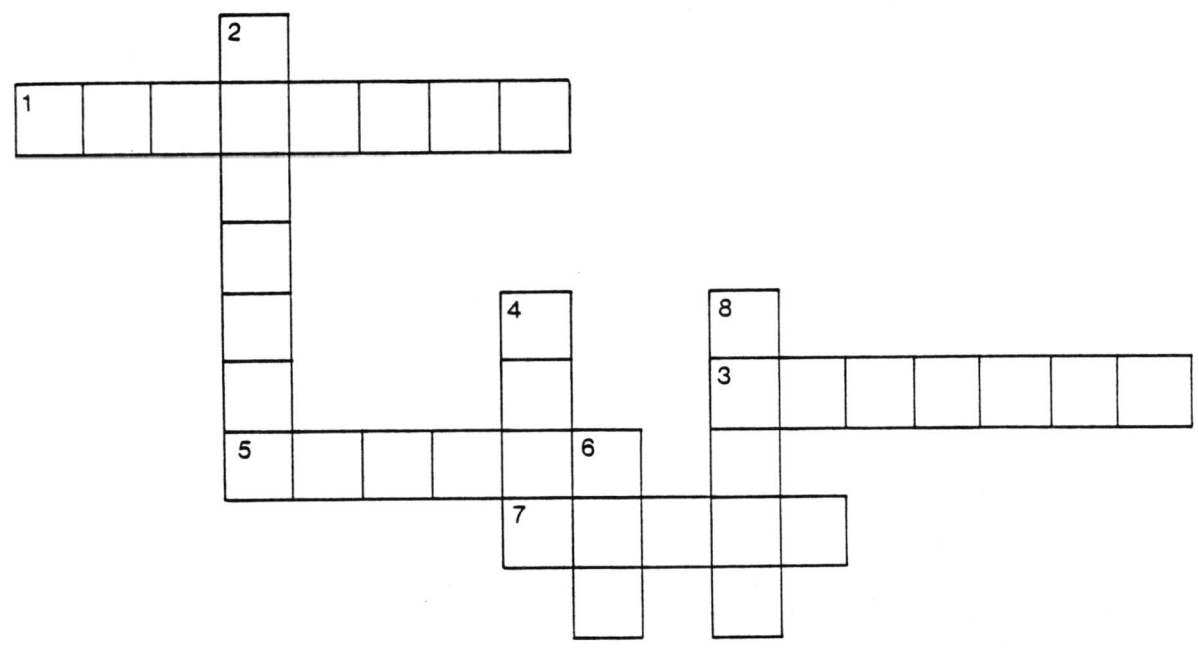

Number Search

Find & complete the numbers in this constellation map by filling in the dotted lines. (Watch out for extra stars that aren't part of the numbers). Then circle the number that answers the question "How many friends do you have in your class?"

Did you count yourself?

"Me and My Classmates" Completion

Complete the following sentences.

1. I have _____ friends at school.

2. My best friend at school is _____ .

3. Most classmates at school think I am _____ .

4. The best time for me to be with my classmates
   is _____ .

5. With regards to my friends at school, I wish

   _____ .

6. The best time I ever had with my friends at
   school was _____ .

"Design a Teacher" Cut Out

Cut out the parts of this teacher that help to complete the sentence "My favorite kind of teacher is _____ ." Place the parts where they belong on this model teacher.

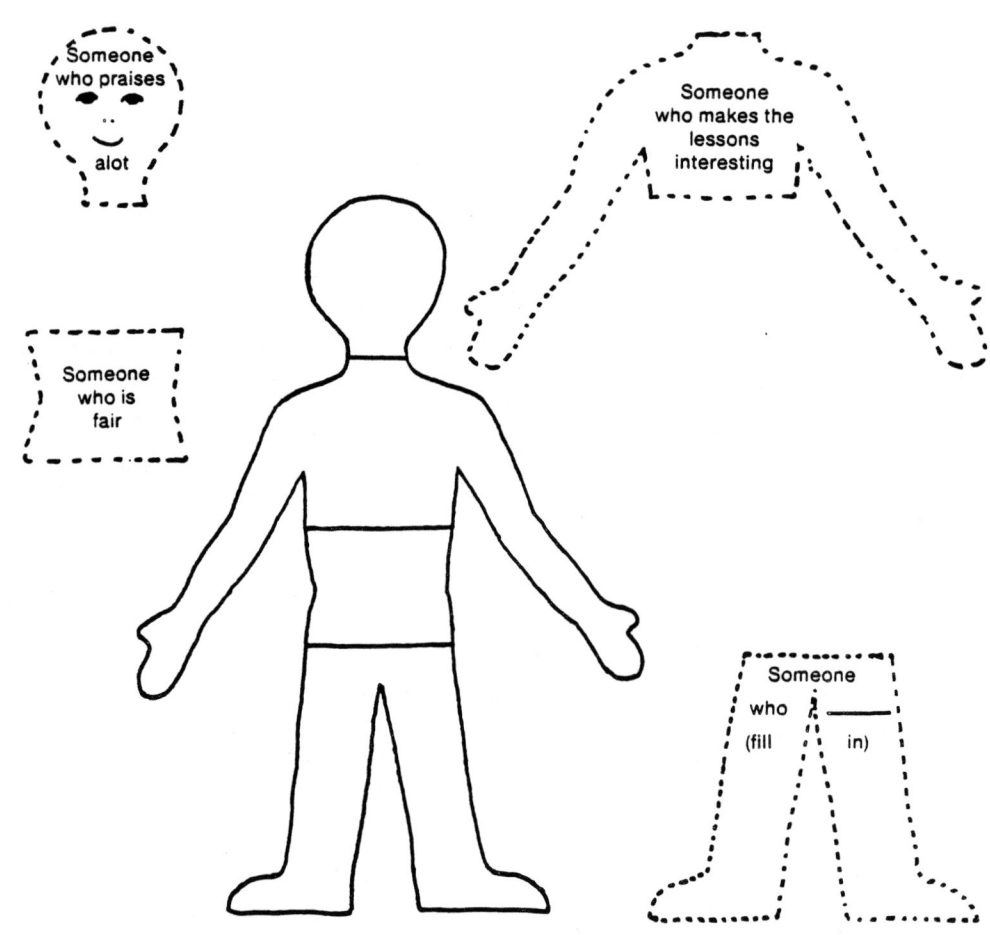

"Me and My Teachers" Completion

Complete the following:

1. "My favorite teacher is _____."

2. "I like this teacher because _____
_____."

3. "I wish my teachers would _____
_____."

4. "The hardest time for me to talk to a teacher is
   ☐ when I am in trouble.
   ☐ when I need help.
   ☐ other _____."

5. I think most teachers are fair to me
   ☐ Yes
   ☐ No

6. Someday I hope I can _____
with my teachers.

"Me as a Student" Completion

This is a calendar showing all the school days this past month. Color all the days you were a good student.

	Monday	Tuesday	Wednesday	Thursday	Friday
Week I					
Week II					
Week III					
Week IV					

How could you have more of these days?

Student-O-Meter

Cut out the arrow and place it on the student-o-meter to show the aspect of school you are the best at.

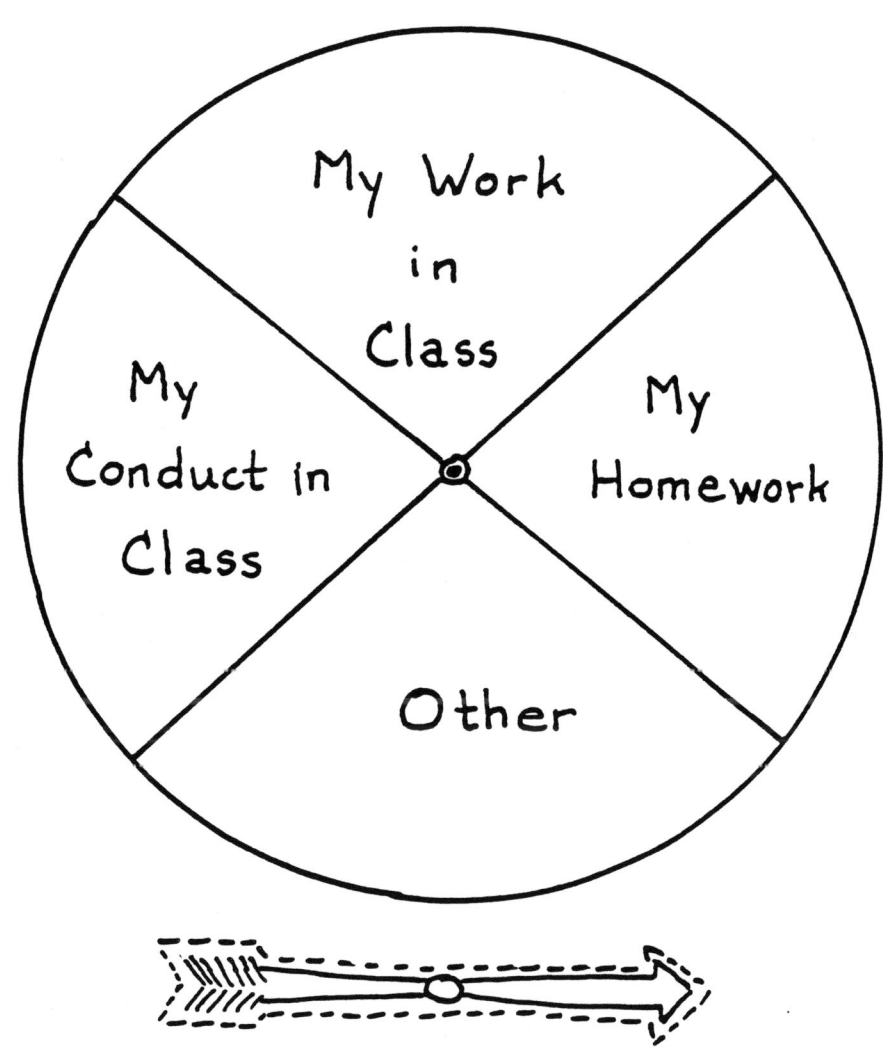

1. Does your student-o-meter change alot from day to day?
2. In what way does it change?
3. Ideally, what would you like it to look like?
4. How can you make that happen?

Picture Completion

You have been given the opportunity to come up with a way to change your school so that you would be happier there. Draw or write in your idea.

How could you make this happen?

Brainstorm Game

Two players write down all the things that make them happy at school on the list below. When the list is finished turn it over. Each player then writes down on another sheet all of the items from the list that they can remember. The player that remembers the most wins!

Happiness at school is...

1._____
2._____
3._____
4._____
5._____
6._____
7._____
8._____
9._____
10._____
11._____
12._____
13._____
14._____
15._____

How can you make sure that these things happen frequently?

"Good Days at School" Path

There are many ways to get to the schoolhouse. Fill in the map with the path that is the best way for you to have a good day at school. You can choose several paths if you wish.

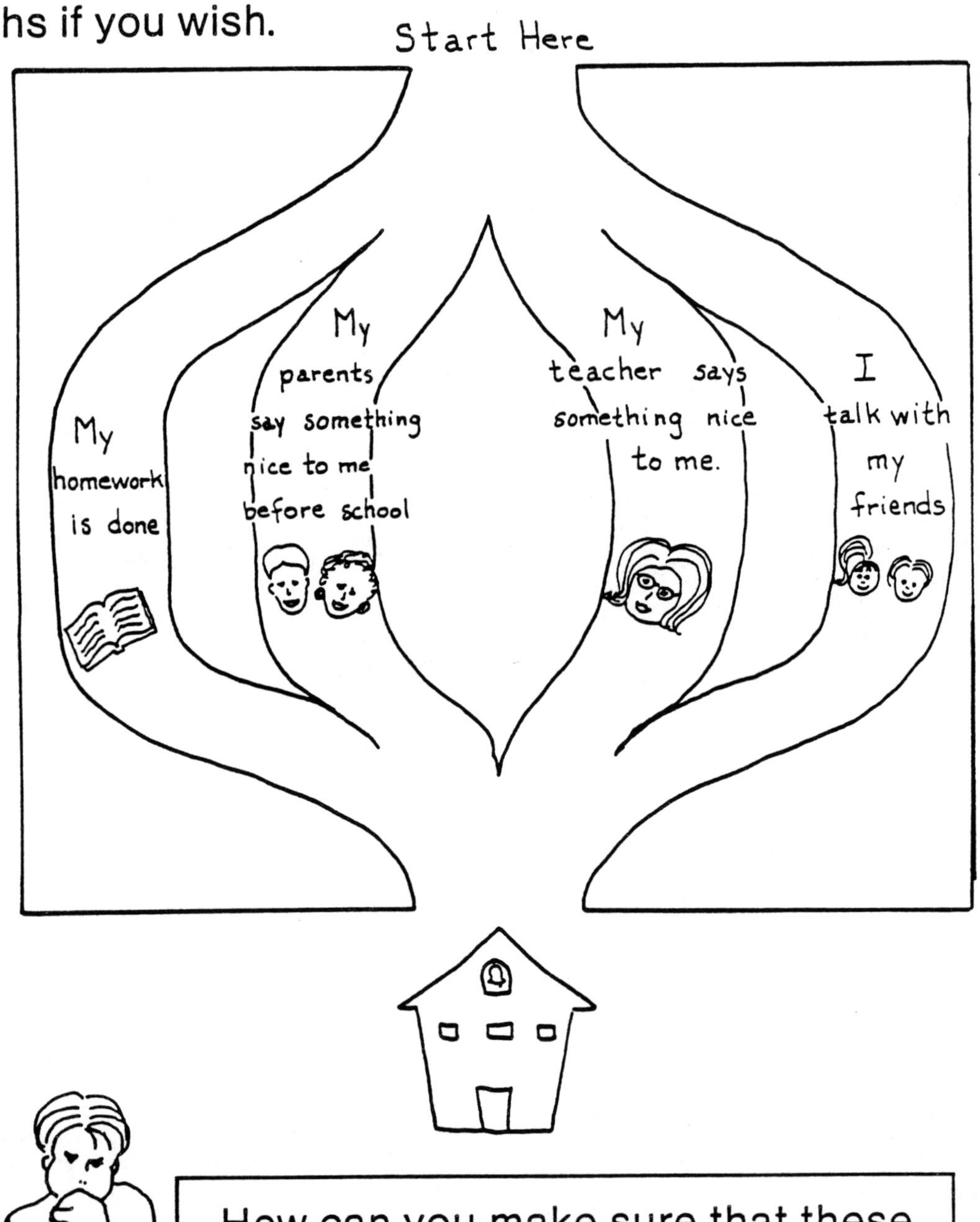

Start Here

My homework is done

My parents say something nice to me before school

My teacher says something nice to me.

I talk with my friends

How can you make sure that these things happen?

Guess What Game

All players are given a copy of this game sheet. Each player writes in the spaces below all the different ways this boy had a good day at school. The player who fills in all the spaces first wins!

"Me and My School Work"
Sentence Completion

Complete the following sentences with a word from the computer screen that best describes your school work.

1. "Usually my school work is _____ when I do it."
2. "I would like to improve my school work so that it is more _____ ."
3. "Even though its important that my work is neat, its more important that it be _____ ."
4. "Even though my work might be _____ and _____ ,its most important that I understand it so that I can use that knowledge in the future."

Opposites Games

Draw a line between the words about school work that are opposites. Circle the words that best describe your school work.

messy	incorrect
confused	low
slowly	school work
printing	misunderstand
high	upset
correct	sad
praised	clear
comprehend	embarrassed
excited	neat
home work	criticized
happy	quickly
proud	cursive

Reading Fill In

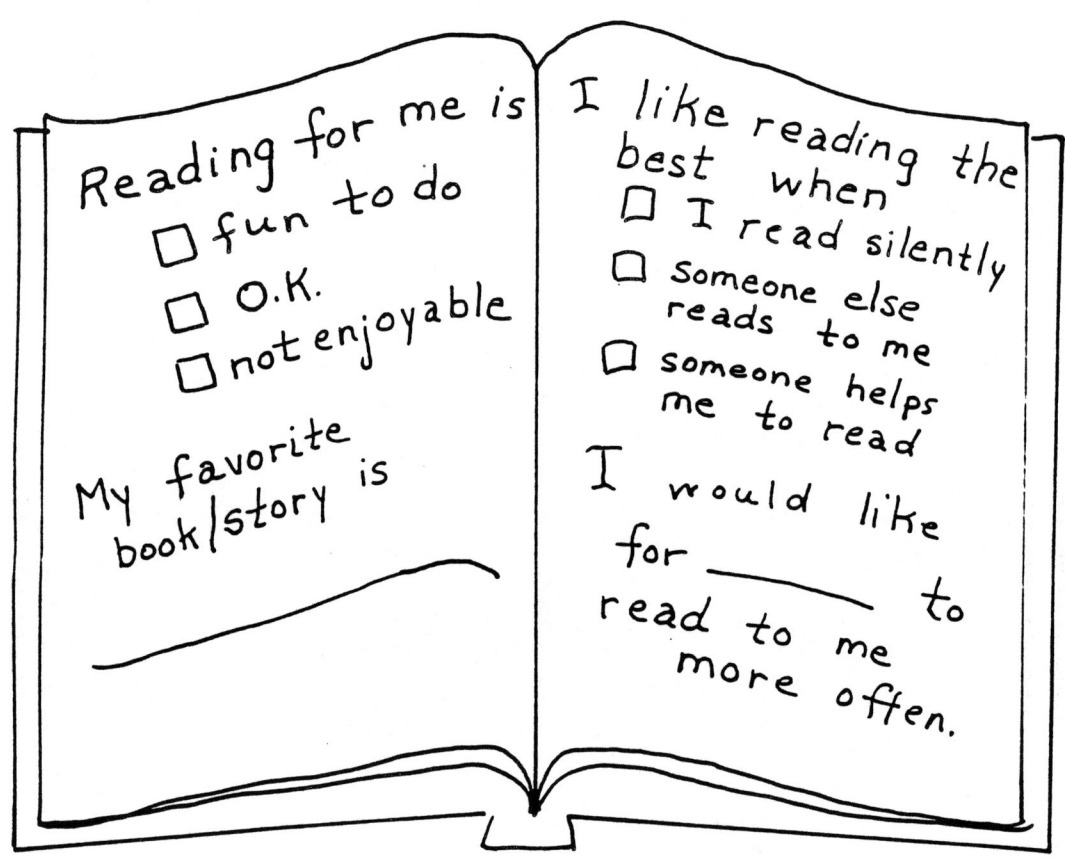

Complete the following:

Reading for me is
- ☐ fun to do
- ☐ O.K.
- ☐ not enjoyable

My favorite
book/story is

_____

I like reading the
best when
- ☐ I read silently
- ☐ Someone else reads to me
- ☐ someone helps me to read

I would like
for _____ to
read to me
more often.

Coded Story

Decode the following story by using the words that go with these pictures:

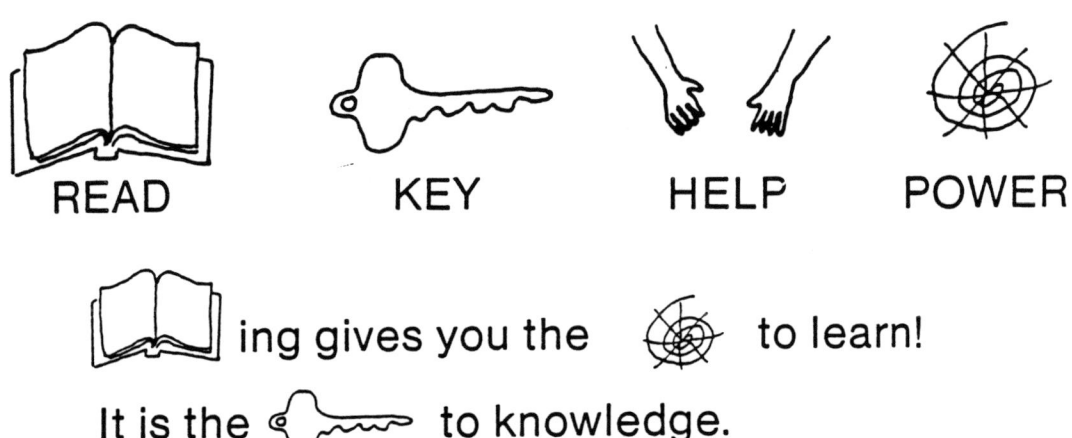

READ   KEY   HELP   POWER

READ ing gives you the POWER to learn!

It is the KEY to knowledge.

Some people enjoy books the most when they READ by themselves. Other people enjoy books when someone else READ s to them. Still other people enjoy books the most when someone HELP s them to READ . It is O.K. to experience some difficulties when you are trying to READ . It is also O.K. to ask for HELP .

When you can READ , you have the POWER to learn. READ ing is like having "the force" on your side!

Maze

Doing math work is like going through this maze. You have to think about it. Draw a path through the maze to reach the questions about math and you.

START ↓

1. "Math for me is
   ☐ easy
   ☐ O.K.
   ☐ hard."

2. "I enjoy math the most when
   ☐ someone helps me
   ☐ I do it myself."

3. "I could do better at math if _____."

Coded Message

✏️ Use the code below to spell out this important message about math.

1	2	3	4	5	6	7	8	9	10	11	12	13	14	15	16	17	18	19	20	21	22	23	24	25	26
A	B	C	D	E	F	G	H	I	J	K	L	M	N	O	P	Q	R	S	T	U	V	W	X	Y	Z

13•1•20•8   3•1•14   2•5   5•1•19•25

__ __ __ __   __ __ __   __ __   __ __ __ __

6•15•18   19•15•13•5   19•20•21•4•5•14•20•19

__ __ __   __ __ __ __   __ __ __ __ __ __ __ __

20•15   12•5•1•18•14   1•14•4   8•1•18•4

__ __   __ __ __ __ __   __ __ __   __ __ __ __

6•15•18   15•20•8•5•18•19.

__ __ __   __ __ __ __ __ __

How can you make math more enjoyable?

Home from School
Picture Completion

Complete this picture by adding what you would like to do or have someone do for you when you get home from school.

Home From School Game

Each player uses coins as game markers & dice. Flip the coin to advance. Heads means that you move ahead one space & tails means two spaces. When you land on a space with a dot on it, you must say one thing you like to do or have done for you when you get home from school. The first player home wins!

211

Take a Walk through Testland

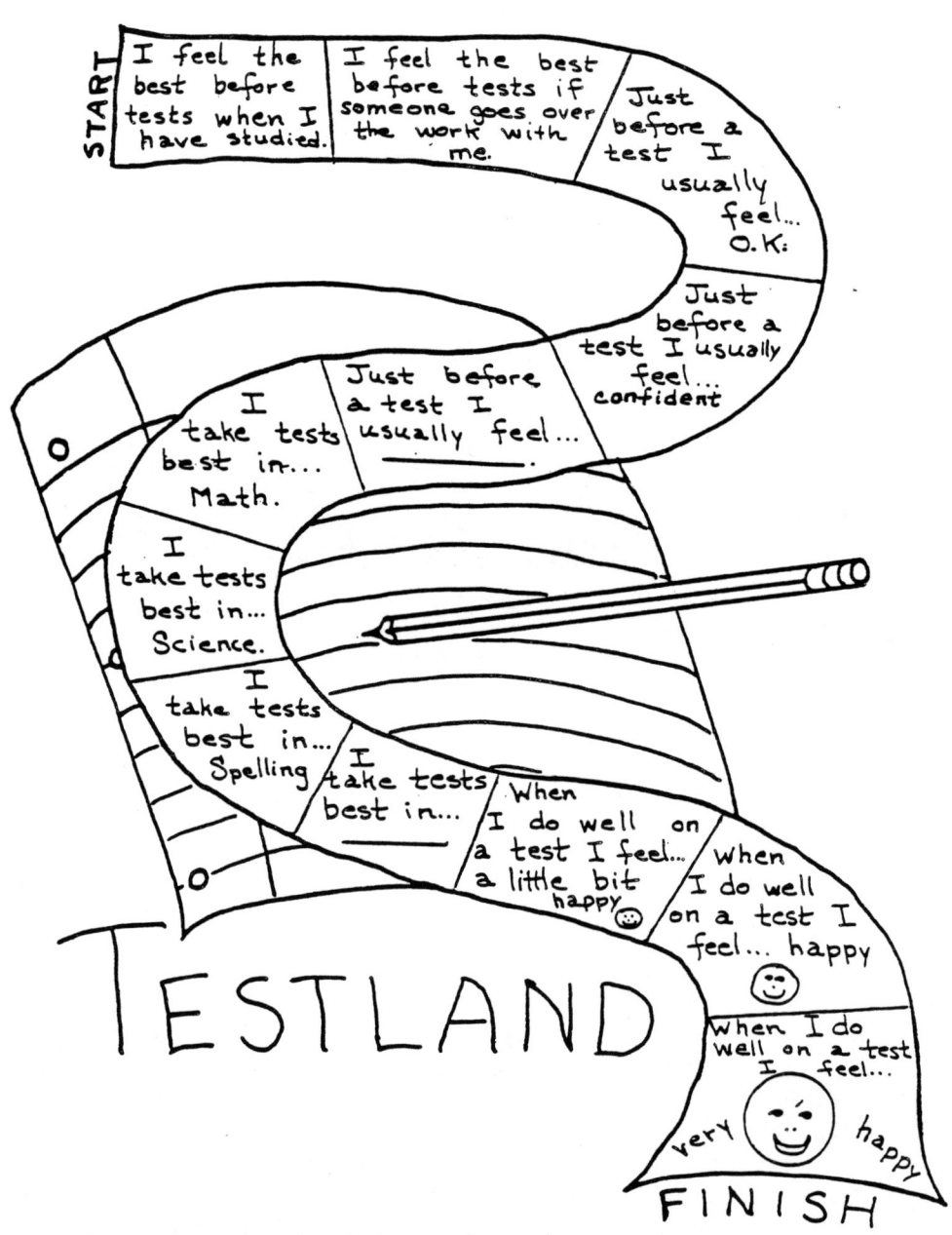 Take a walk through testland and color in the steps along the way that apply to you.

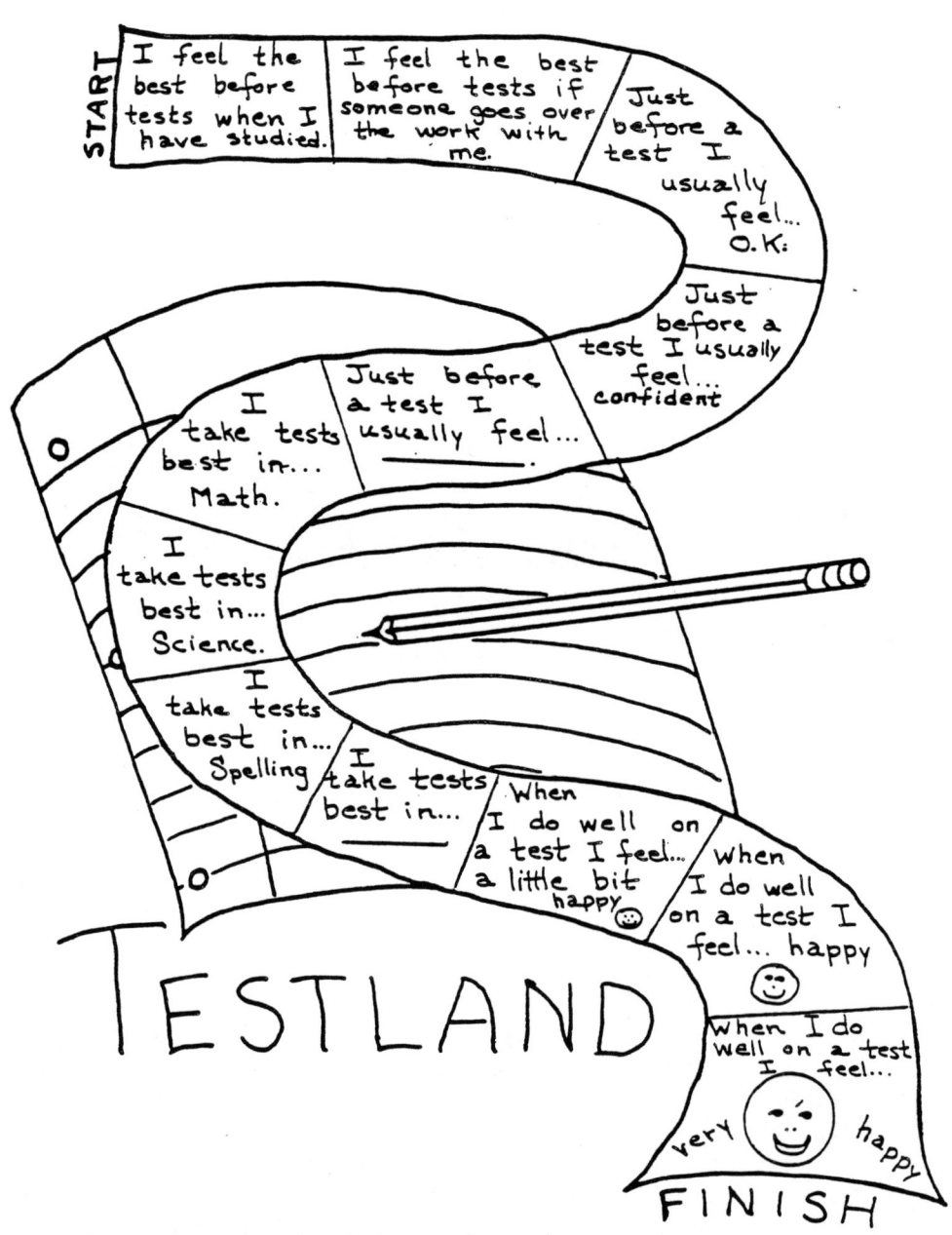

START

I feel the best before tests when I have studied.

I feel the best before tests if someone goes over the work with me.

Just before a test I usually feel... O.K.

Just before a test I usually feel... confident

Just before a test I usually feel... _____

I take tests best in... Math.

I take tests best in... Science.

I take tests best in... Spelling

I take tests best in...

When I do well on a test I feel... a little bit happy

When I do well on a test I feel... happy

When I do well on a test I feel... very happy

TESTLAND

FINISH

Report Card Fill In

Write in the grades & teachers comments that you would like to see yourself get on a report card on the form below.

Name —————————
Days Present —————
Days Absent —————
Days Tardy —————
Teachers Comments:
—————————
—————————
—————————

Spelling —————————
Reading —————————
Math —————————
Science —————————
Social Studies —————
Writing —————————
Phys Ed. —————————
Other —————————

How do you decide if your grades have improved?

What's Wrong?

Find and circle three situations in the picture below that make a school day get off to a bad start. What gets your school day off to a bad start?

Word Matching Game

Draw a line between the words below that are similar. All of these words have to do with bad days at school. Then circle the words that describe ways you have had bad days at school.

often	not once
yell	guardians
sick	argue/hit
tired	make fun
parents	instructor
night	not neat
teacher	evening
teased	frequently
fight	AM
never	scream
messy	not feeling well
morning	sleepy

"Getting Help" Completion

Check the answers that fit best for you. Then color the important message below.

1.) "I ask for help with my work
☐ whenever I need to
☐ not often enough
☐ too often."

2.) "When I ask for help at school I feel...
☐ O.K.
☐ embarrassed
☐ other."

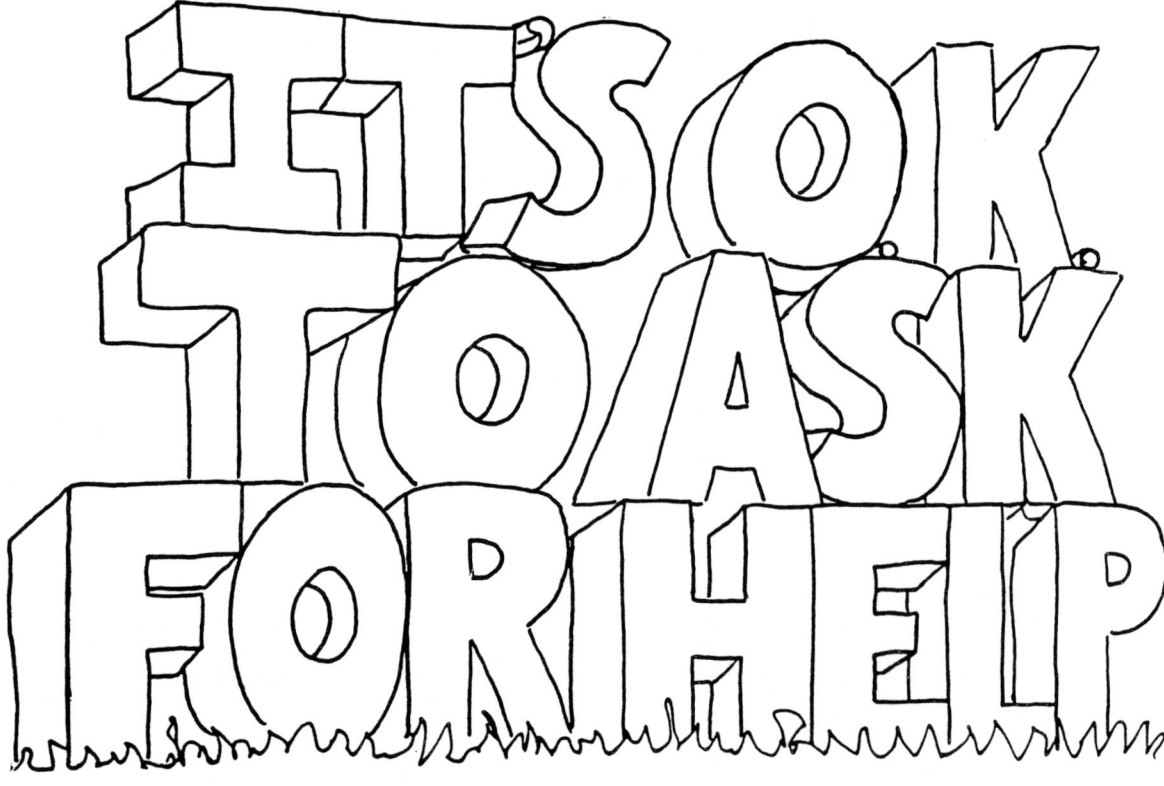

Feeling Proud at School

Cut out the blocks and place them on the letter "P" to show some of the ways that people feel proud at school. Circle the blocks that tell the ways that you feel proud at school. Fill in the empty blocks with other ways to feel proud.

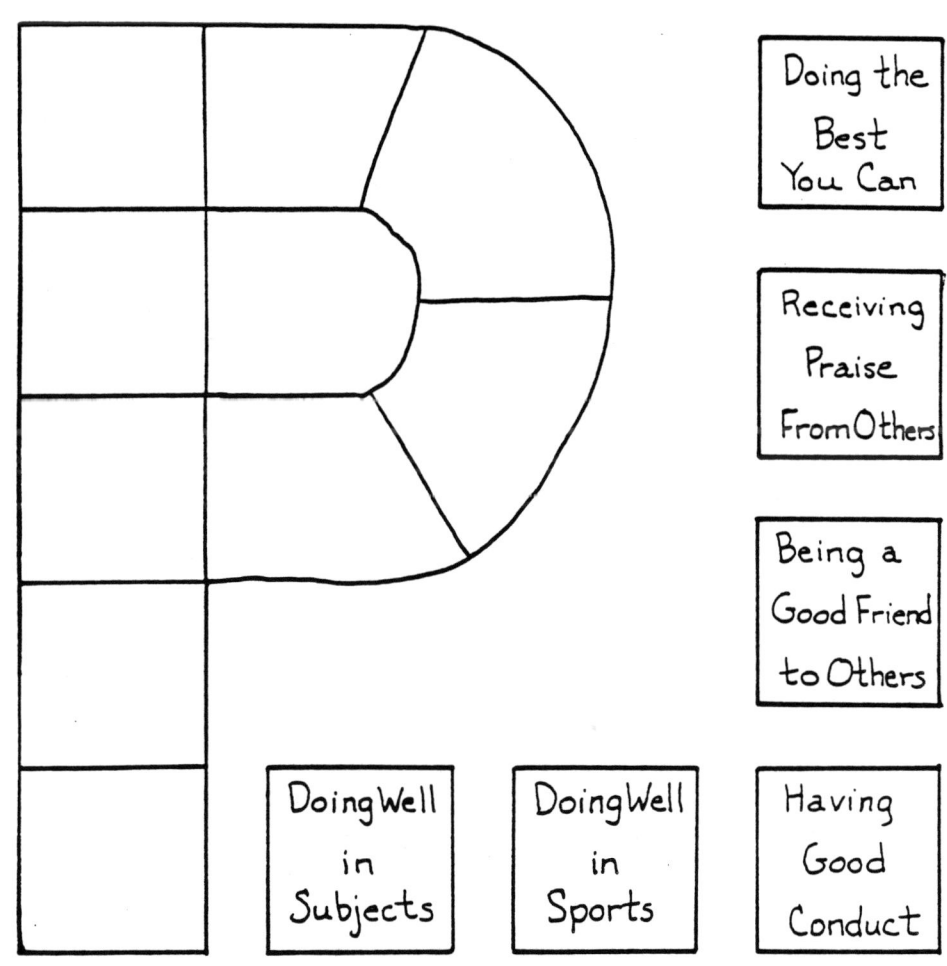

Doing the Best You Can

Receiving Praise From Others

Being a Good Friend to Others

Doing Well in Subjects

Doing Well in Sports

Having Good Conduct

Saying Goodbye Sentence Completion

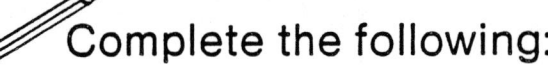 Complete the following:

1. "I have left _____ schools."

2. "The teacher I miss the most is _____ ."

3. "When I say goodbye at the end of each year, I feel

☐ happy    ☐ sad

☐ O.K.    ☐ other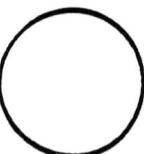

What can you do to feel good about saying good-bye at the end of the school year?

Picture Fill In

Leaving a school that you like can be sad. If you had to leave your school, think of all the parts that you would miss the most and write them in the sections of the heart below.

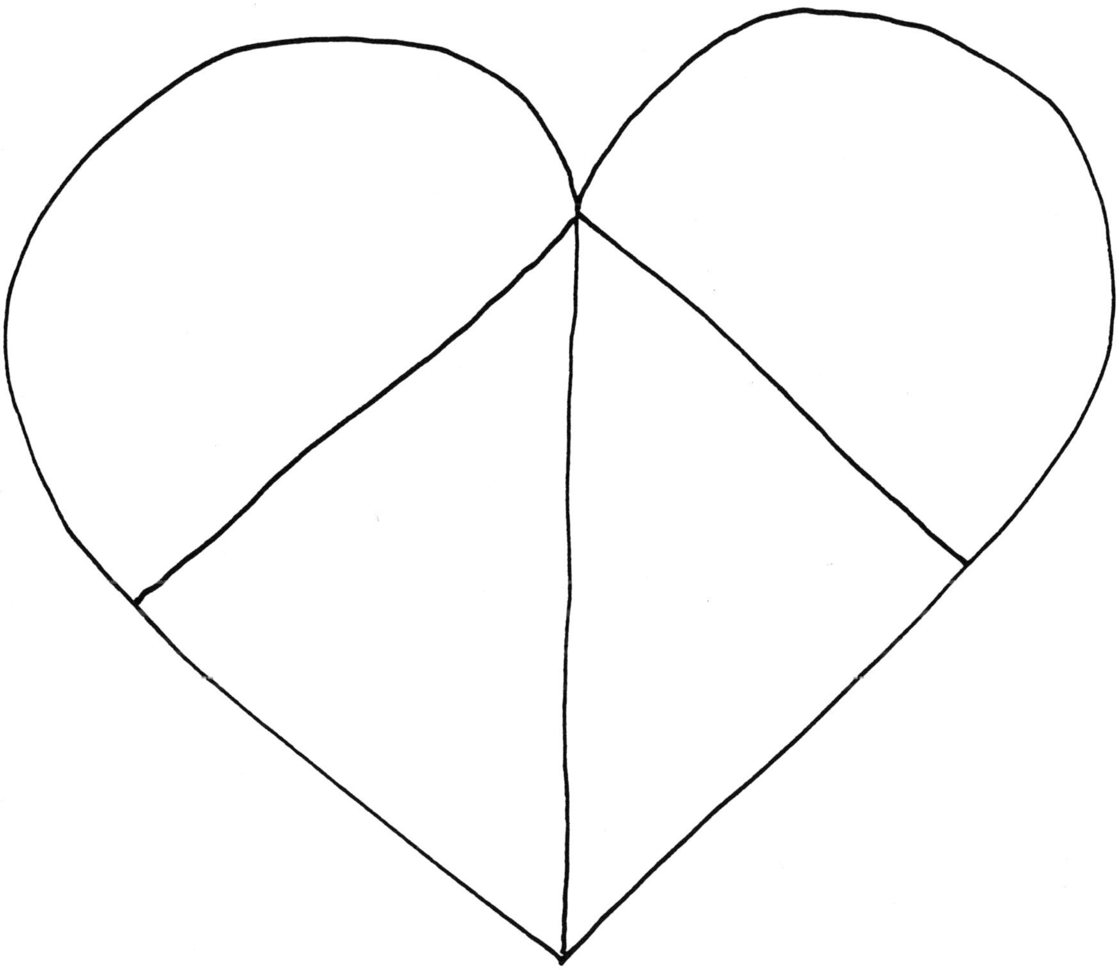

How can you show appreciation for those parts of school?

CHAPTER EIGHT

ACTIVITIES RELATED TO TERMINATION
AND FOLLOW-UP

IN THIS CHAPTER, the reader will find activities related to the termination of therapy and follow-up sessions. Clinicians need to use interventions such as these to provide closure to the therapeutic relationship. Counselors will find that some of these activities are appropriate to use when checking up on former clients in follow-up sessions. As always, these more structured and game-like plans make an issue like termination more comfortable to address. Readers will find that these activities help children acknowledge the progress they have made in treatment, work through their grief about termination, and begin to explore other sources of support. The follow-up activities assist in evaluating what changes the child has maintained and identify problems that have surfaced subsequent to the termination of therapy.

In Table XII, Themes for Activities Related to Termination and Follow-up, the reader will find themes listed for all the activities in this chapter. Clinicians should refer to this table for selecting appropriate themes for a child in the final phase of treatment.

TABLE XII

THEMES FOR ACTIVITIES RELATED TO TERMINATION AND FOLLOW-UP

PAGE	ACTIVITY	THEME
224 225	Picture Completion Opposites Game	Exploring child's feelings about termination with therapist
226 227	Word Jumble Do You Remember?	Reviewing positive aspects of the therapeutic relationship
228 229	Picture Fill-in Sentence Completion	Getting child to disclose the value of therapeutic relationship
230 231	Word Search Word Scramble Sentence Completion	Having child reflect on personal changes in therapy
232 233	Feelings Completion Opposites Game	Reviewing affective growth with child
234 235	Picture Completion "Me and My Parents" Completion	Exploring changes in child's relationship with parents
236 237	"Me and My Friends Now" Picture Completion "My Friends" Computer Program	Reviewing progress made regarding child's social skills
238 239	Picture Completion "S" Board Game	Having child reflect on change in his/her interactions with peers
240 241	Awards Fill-in Word Matching Game	Exploring child's perception of his/her changes at school
242 243	Sentence Completion Connect Game	Reflecting on child's increased self-confidence

TABLE XII *(continued)*

THEMES FOR ACTIVITIES RELATED TO TERMINATION AND FOLLOW-UP

PAGE	ACTIVITY	THEME
244	Picture Fill-in	Exploring sources of support for a child
245	Brainstorm Game	
246	"A New Me"	Reviewing major changes child has accomplished
247	Word Completion Game	
248	Word Find	Child reflecting on previous good-byes
249	Code Game	
250	Crossword Puzzle	Exploring ways child can make his/her happiness
251	Brainstorm and Remember Game	
252	"This is My Life Now"	Having child share view of his/her present life

Picture Completion

Complete the picture below showing how you feel about ending this relationship.

Opposites Game

Draw a line between the words below that are opposites. Then circle the words that describe how you are feeling about leaving.

happy	confident
participate	talk
love	ok
scared	compliment
remember	push away
receive	forget
upset	sad
together	withdraw
criticize	give
listen	hate
hug	separate

Word Jumble

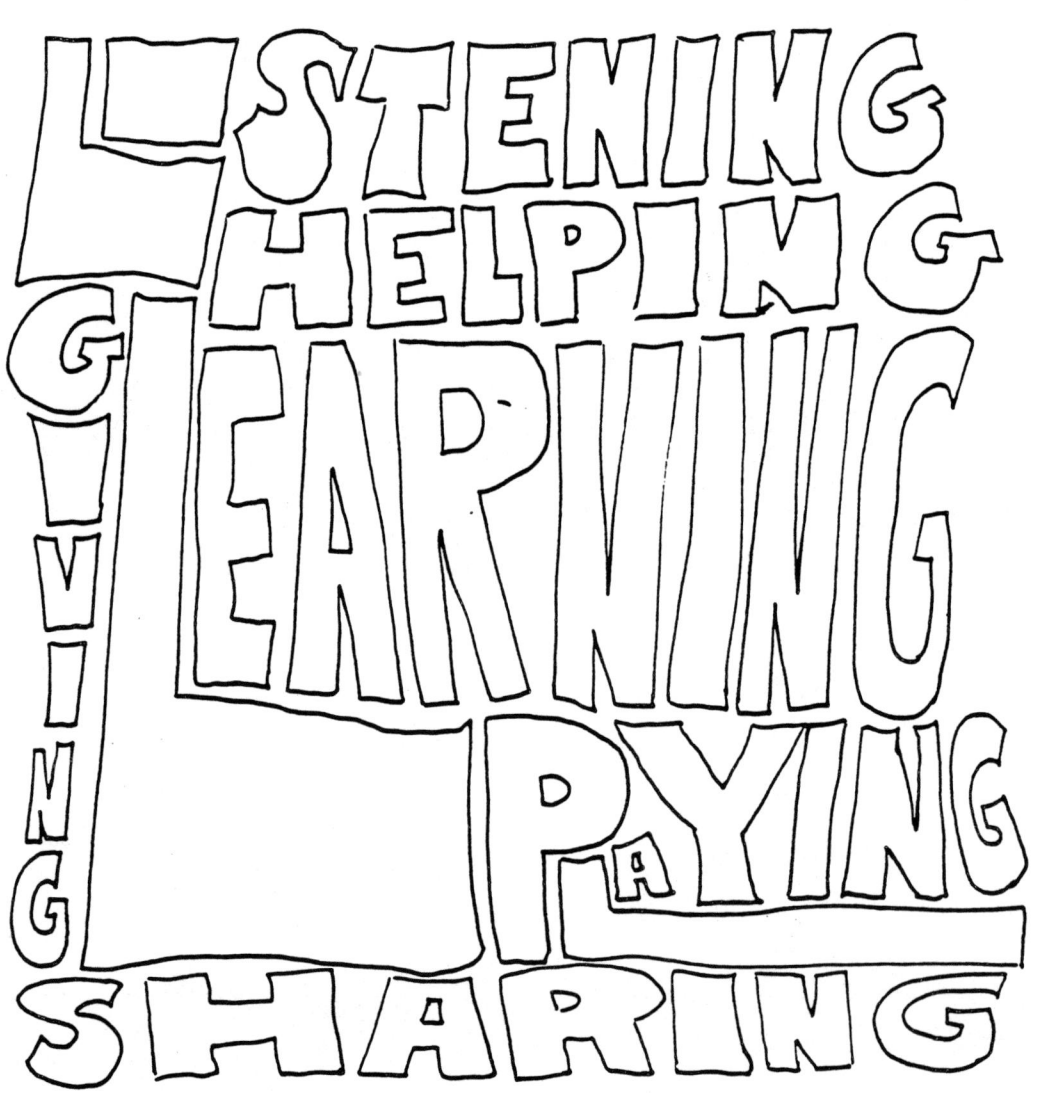

The words in this word jumble all have to do with the friendship that has developed during this relationship. Find all six and color each one a different color.

Do You Remember?

Each player uses one of the sheets below. Begin by writing all the different things each player has learned about the other during this friendship. The player that thinks of the most things after 5 minutes wins.

Things I have learned about You:	Things I have learned about You:
_____	_____
_____	_____
_____	_____
_____	_____
_____	_____
_____	_____
_____	_____
_____	_____
_____	_____

Player _____ | Player _____

Picture Fill-In

Imagine that you have been given 6 robots that will do everything for you that your therapist/teacher used to do for you. Write or draw on the 6 robots everything that you will miss about this relationship.

Which one is most important to you?

Sentence Completion

Put a check in the box that answers these questions the best for you.

1. "This relationship has been good for me in many ways   ☐ Yes
    ☐ Maybe
    ☐ No."

2. "The best part of the relationship for me has been...
    ☐ the friendship   ☐ the learning
    ☐ the games   ☐ other."

3. "The activity I enjoyed the most here was _____."

4. "I feel I have been a nice person to work with every week.   ☐ Yes
    ☐ Maybe
    ☐ No."

5. "The feeling I have about ending this relationship is...
    ☐ Sad   ☐ Happy and Sad
    ☐ Afraid   ☐ Other."

Word Search

Circle all the words that have to do with ways in which you may feel better about yourself. Then color the circled words that describe the things that apply to you. See if you can find all ten words.

```
S F R I E N D S P
P L A Y I N G F A
T E W S I S T E R
E H O M E F U N E
A B R O T H E R N
D A K G A M E S T
H M S C H O O L S
```

Word Scramble Sentence Completion

Unscramble the following words to complete the sentences correctly. Then circle the sentences that describe ways in which you feel better about yourself.

1. "I nkow _____ myself alot ettbre _____."

2. "I eefl _____ more fidneceonc _____."

3. "I feel better baotu _____ lapying _____ with my rfnieds _____."

4. "I feel ebttre _____ about my hooscl owrk _____ _____."

5. "I own _____ ikel _____ myself alot omre _____."

Feelings Completion

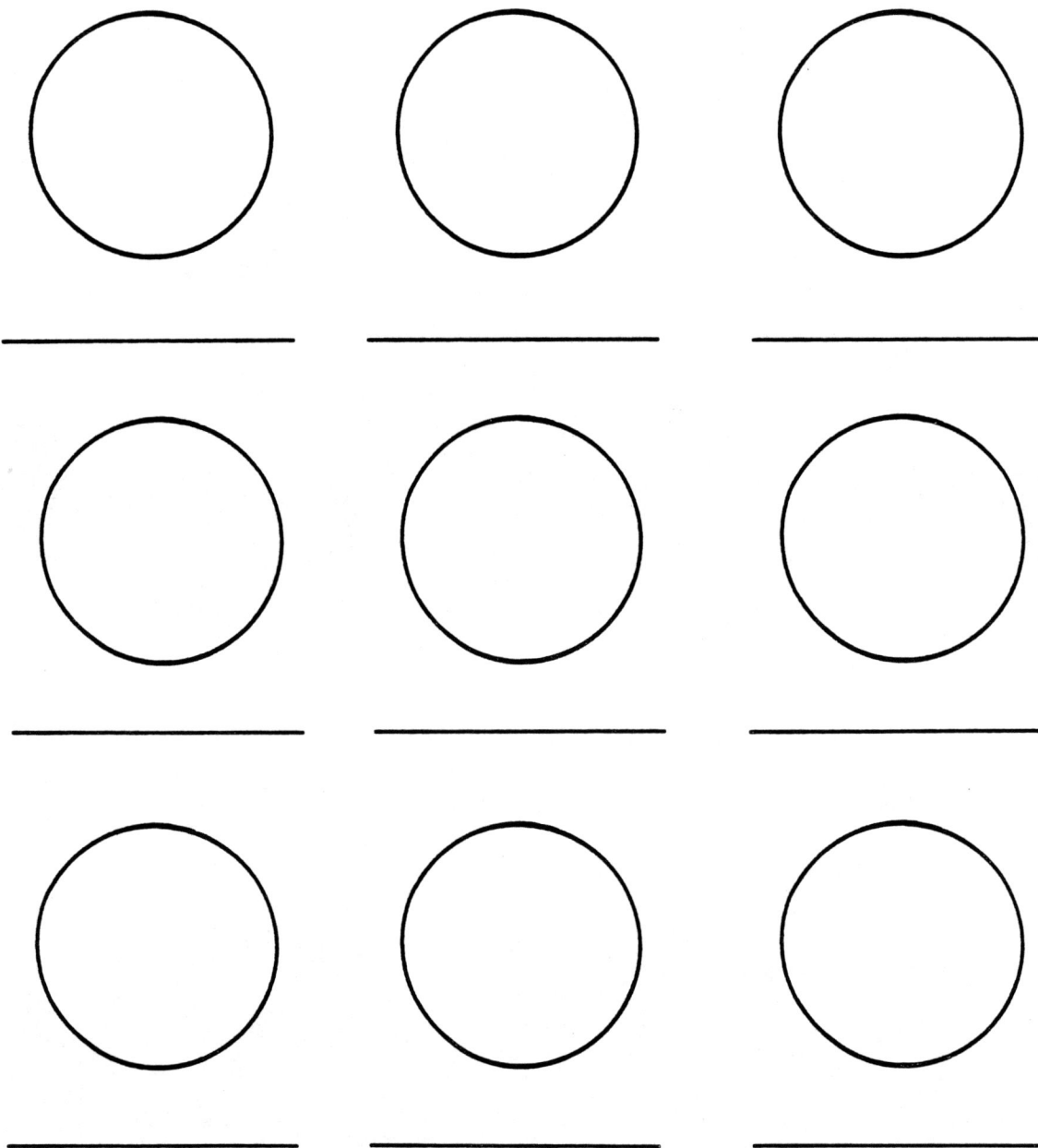

See how many different feelings you can draw on the faces below. Then spell the names of the feelings in the spaces provided.

Opposites Game

Draw a line between the words below that are opposites. All these words have to do with changes you may have made in knowing & sharing your feelings. Circle the words that apply to you.

share	unaware
child	agree
angry	play
more	happy
slowly	friend
dad	adult
sad	talk
work	withhold
stranger	less
know	friendly
disagree	mom
listen	quickly

Picture Completion

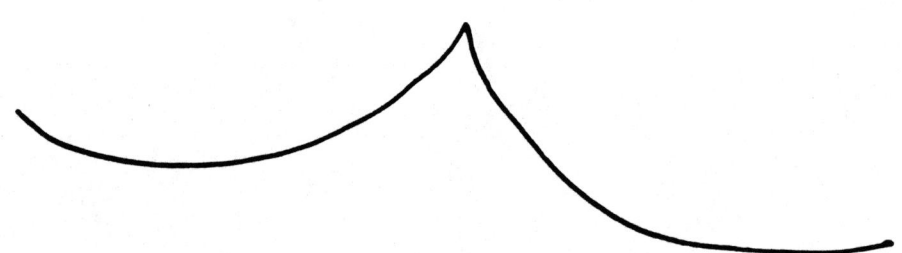

Complete this picture so that it has something to do with you and your family now.

"Me and My Parents Completion"

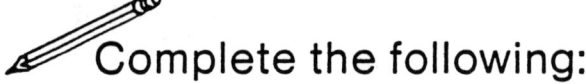Complete the following:

1. "My parents and I feel _____ ."

2. "I am doing better with my parents because _____ ."

3. "My parents like the way I now _____ ."

4. "One thing I want to improve with my parents is _____ ."

5. "My parents are great about _____ ."

6. "My parents are lucky to have me because _____ ."

"Me and My Friends Now" Picture Completion

Draw two pictures of yourself with your friends. The first one should show you with your friends before this relationship. The second one should show the changes you have made in the way you get along with friends since this relationship.

Before

Now

"My Friends" Computer Program

Pretend someone else is going to take your place for one week. Leave a message on the computer about the friends you have and what kinds of things you do with them.

1. The friend to play with in my neighborhood is _____ .

2. The friend to play with at school is _____ .

3. The friend who will help you out when you need it is _____ .

4. The friend to talk with about your problems is _____ .

5. Your best friend is _____ .

6. The types of things you do with your friends _____ _____ .

Picture Completion

The pictures below all have to do with your playing skills. Circle the picture that shows your most improved playing skill. Put an X on the picture that shows your least improved skill. Then use your best coloring skills to color all of the pictures.

I enjoy playing with friends.

I play with alot of friends.

I have friends for a long time.

I play fairly and with few fights.

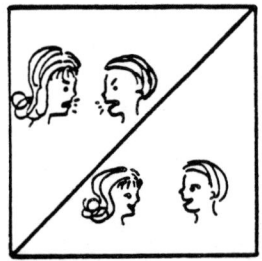

I make up with friends after a fight.

Other _____
_____

"S" Board Game

Each player uses a coin as a game marker and die. Flip the coin to advance. "Heads" means that you move ahead one space and "Tails" means two spaces. Before each player moves their marker, they must say one thing that is better now about their relationships with their friends. If a player forgets to share before they move, they lose their turn. The player that finishes first wins.

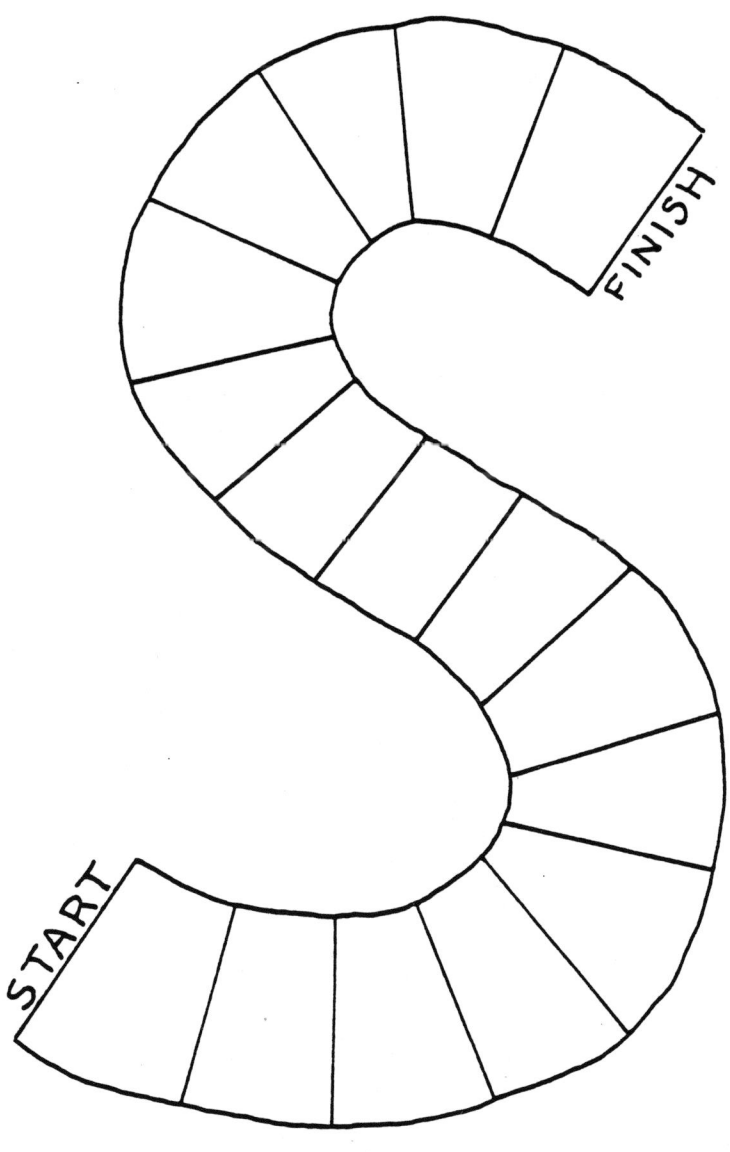

Awards Fill-In

Fill in the award to yourself for the biggest improvements you have made at school this year.

School Improvements for
the Year _____

This is to certify that _____

has been given this award because _____

_____

_____

_____

_____

Signed

_____

Principal

Word Matching Game

Draw a line between the words that are similar. Then circle the words that describe how you are doing or feeling at school now.

dislike	like
well	wonderful
confident	hard
enjoy	understand
easy	desire
happy	hate
great	not difficult
comprehend	sure
difficult	very good
want	delighted

Sentence Completion

Draw a line from the sentence to the word that fits in the blank space. Then circle the sentences that describe ways you feel more confident about yourself.

1. "I try new tasks and _____ on my own."   making

2. "I accept _____ mistakes and know   myself
   that noone can be perfect."

3. "I easily give and _____ compliments."   receive

4. "I stand up for _____ around other kids."   games

5. "I share my _____ with both children   feelings
   and adults."

Can you think of any other ways you are feeling more confident about yourself?

Connect Game

Each player takes a turn connecting one or two dots as their move. Before a player connects their dots, they must share one thing they feel more self confident about. If a player forgets to share, they lose a turn. The player to cross out the last dot wins!

Picture Fill-In

Write the names of people or things that could help this boy, on each of the balloons. Think of people or things that have been helping you lately when you needed help.

Brainstorm Game

Two players take 10 minutes and brainstorm together about all the people that could help a kid out. Write down all the names on the sheet. Feel free to include your friends' names. Then turn the sheet over. Both players write down on another sheet as many names from the list as they can remember. The player who remembers the most wins.

> **People who could help a kid**
>
> _____
>
> _____
>
> _____
>
> _____
>
> _____
>
> _____
>
> _____
>
> _____
>
> _____
>
> _____

"A New Me"

Complete this picture of yourself. Draw your face today. Write or draw four major changes you have made in the last six months in the boxes below.

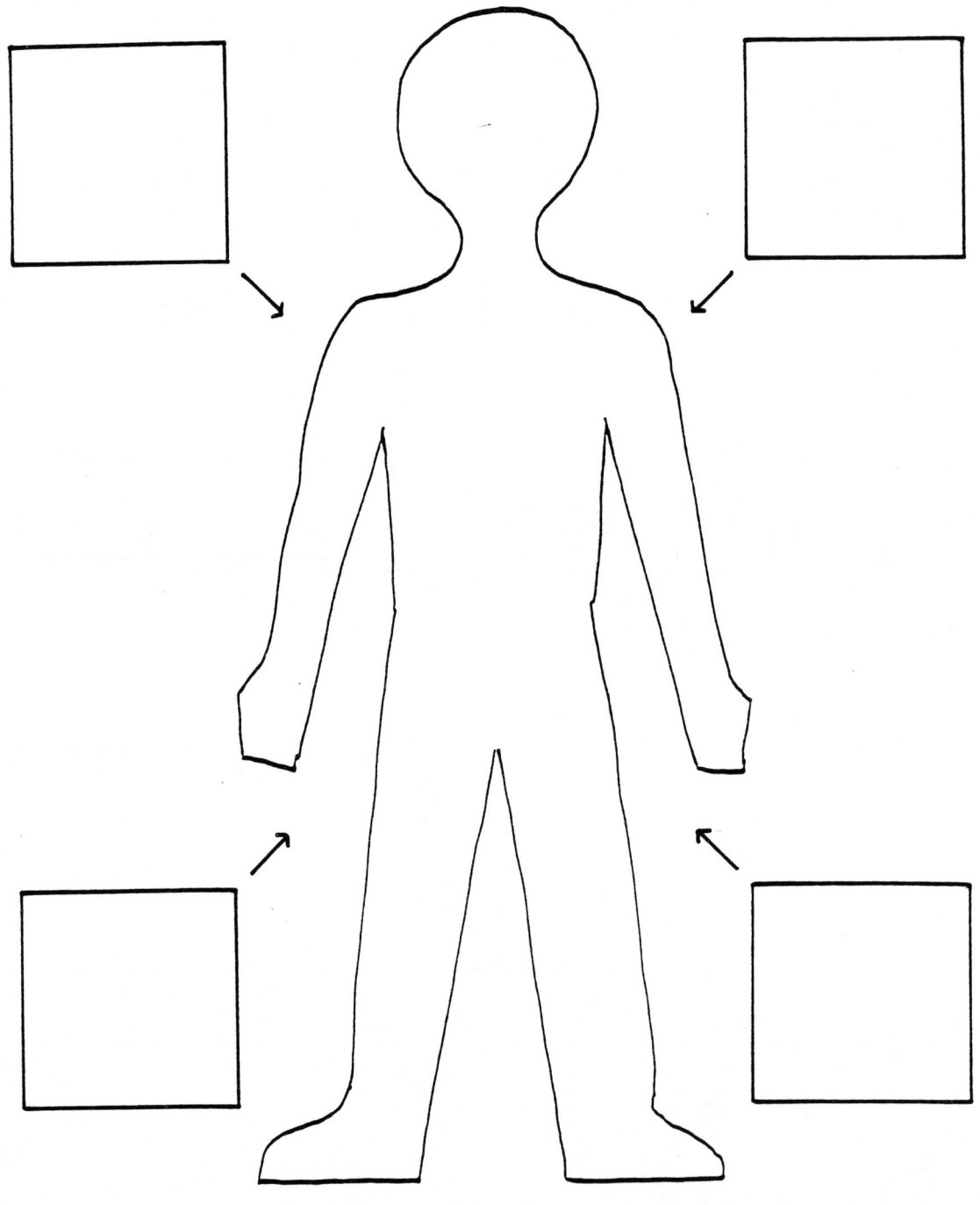

Word Completion Game

Use the letters from the word "yourself" to list changes you have made recently. The word or phrase must begin with the letter on each line.

Y _____

O _____

U _____

R _____

S _____

E _____

L _____

F _____

Other changes _____

Word Find

Saying goodbye to someone special often reminds us of other times we have had to say goodbye. Circle all the words in this word find that are names of people. Then go back & circle in red the names of the people that you have had to say goodbye to in the past.

The letters form a large "G" shape containing hidden words:

motherzeryphstltiuv
grandfatherti
tojerzkcounselor
dadlov
sistergrandmotherjolemot
zxeu
plefg
cherz
teacher
timltminister
brotheriltibelrmuzle/oq
uncle/fe
doctori
albaunt
neighbor
cfriendxyi
abrabbiet
retloi

Code Game

Use the code below to spell out this message.

1	2	3	4	5	6	7	8	9	10	11	12	13	14	15	16	17	18	19	20	21	22	23	24	25	26
A	B	C	D	E	F	G	H	I	J	K	L	M	N	O	P	Q	R	S	T	U	V	W	X	Y	Z

19•1•25•9•14•7

— — — — — —

7•15•15•4•2•25•5   20•15

— — — — — — —   — —

19•15•13•5•15•14•5   19•16•5•3•9•1•12

— — — — — — —   — — — — — — —

18•5•13•9•14•4•19   21•19   15•6

— — — — — — —   — —   — —

15•20•8•5•18   7•15•15•4•2•25•5•19.

— — — — —   — — — — — — — —

Name the ones you remember _____

_____

249

Crossword Puzzle

Fill in the crossword puzzle using the clues. All of the answers have to do with possible ways you can take care of yourself and be happy. Circle the ones that apply to you.

Across

1. Vegetables, fruit, bread, etc.

3. Do for others

5. Go through a book

7. Do what parents & teachers say

8. Put on your own clothes

Down

2. Work that you bring from school

4. Mom & Dad

6. In bed at night

Brainstorm and Remember Game

You and another player use the sheet below to brainstorm all the ways you have found to take care of yourself. Turn the list over and set a timer at 3 minutes. Both players try to list on another sheet of paper as many items from the list that they can remember. The player that remembers the most wins!

Ways I Can Take Care of Myself

1. _____

2. _____

3. _____

4. _____

5. _____

6. _____

7. _____

8. _____

9. _____

10. _____

11. _____

12. _____

"This Is My Life Now"

Draw a picture that shows what your life is like now.

APPENDICES

APPENDIX A

SUPPLEMENTAL READING MATERIAL

Child Development

1. Adock, Don and Segal, Marilyn: *Play and Learning.* Rolling Hills Estates, Calif., B. L. Winch, 1979.
2. Ambron, Sueann Robinson: *Child Development.* New York, Holt, Rinehart and Winston, 1981.
3. Ames, Louise and Gessel, Arnold: *The Child From Five to Ten.* New York, Harper & Row, 1977.
4. Bemporad, Jules R.: *Child Development in Normality and Psychopathology.* New York, Brunner-Mazel, 1980.
5. Best, Raphaela: *We've All Got Scars: What Boys and Girls Learn in Elementary School.* Bloomington, Indiana University Press, 1983.
6. Brooks-Gunn, Jeanne and Schempp-Matthews, Wendy: *He & She: How Children Develop Their Sex-Role Identity.* Englewood Cliffs, Prentice-Hall, 1979.
7. Butler, Annie Louise; Gotts, Edward Earl; and Quisenberry, Nancy L.: *Play as Development.* Columbus, Ohio, Merrill, 1978.
8. Damon, William: *Social and Personality Development: Infancy Through Adolescence.* New York, W. W. Norton, 1983.
9. Griffore, Robert J.: *Child Development: An Educational Perspective.* Springfield, Charles C Thomas, 1981.
10. Ilg, Frances L. and Bates Ames, Louise: *Child Behavior.* New York, Harper & Row, 1955, 1966, 1977.
11. Nagera, Humberto: *A Developmental Approach to Childhood Psychopathology.* New York, Jason Aronson, 1981.
12. Rexford, Eveoleen N. (Ed.): *A Developmental Approach to Problems of Acting Out.* New York, International Universities Press, 1978.
13. Sarnoff, Charles: *Latency.* New York, Jason Aronson, 1976.
14. Wolman, Benjamin: *Manual of Child Psychopathology.* New York, McGraw-Hill, 1972.
15. Worell, Judith: *Psychological Development in the Elementary Years.* New York, Academic Press, 1982.

Assessment of Children for Therapy

1. Barkley, Russell A.: *Hyperactive Children: A Handbook for Diagnosis and Treatment.* New York, Guilford, 1981.

2. Boyle, Michael H. and Lowes, Sharon C.: Selecting measures of emotional and behavioral disorders of childhood for use in general populations. *Journal for Child Psychology and Psychiatry, 26,* 137-159, 1985.

3. Cronbach, Lee J.: *Essentials of Psychological Testing.* New York, Harper & Row, 1970.

4. Dileo, Joseph: *Childrens Drawing as Diagnostic Aids.* New York, Brunner/Mazel, 1973.

5. Dileo, Joseph: *Young Children and Their Drawings.* New York, Brunner/Mazel, 1970.

6. Goldman, Leo: *Using Tests in Counseling.* New York, Appleton-Century-Crofts, 1971.

7. Herjanic, Barbara; Herjanic, Marijan; Brown, Freeman; and Wheatt, Theotis: Are children reliable reporters? *Journal of Abnormal Child Psychology, 3,* 41-48, 1975.

8. Herjanic, Barbara and Campbell, William: Differentiating psychiatrically disturbed children on the basis of a structured interview. *Journal of Abnormal Child Psychology, 5,* 127-134, 1977.

9. Hobbs, Nicholas: *Futures of Children and Issues in Classification of Children,* Vol. 1 and 2. San Francisco, Jossey-Bass, 1975.

10. Johnson, Orva G. and Bommarito, James W.: *Tests and Measurements in Child Development: Handbook.* San Francisco, Jossey-Bass, 1971.

11. Kazdin, Alan E.: Assessment techniques for childhood depression. *American Academy of Child Psychiatry, 20,* 358-375, 1981.

12. Love, Harold D.: *Psychological Evaluation of Exceptional Children.* Springfield, Charles C Thomas, 1985.

13. Mash, Eric J. and Terdel, Leif G. (Eds.): *Behavioral Assessment of Childhood Disorders.* New York, Guilford, 1984.

14. Powers, Michael D. and Handleman, Jan S.: *Behavioral Assessment of Severe Developmental Disorders.* Rockville, Aspen Systems, 1984.

15. Quay, Herbert C.: *Psychopathological Disorders of Childhood.* New York, John Wiley and Sons, 1979.

16. Rapport, Judith and Ismoud, Deborah: *DSM III Training Guide for Diagnosis of Childhood Disorders.* New York, Brunner/Mazel, 1982.

17. Siegel, Miriam: *Psychological Testing of Children from Preschool Through Adolescence: A Psychodynamic Approach.* New York, International Universities Press, 1984.

18. Slater, Barbara R., and Thomas, John M.: *Psychodiagnostic Evaluation of Children: A Casebook Approach.* New York, Teachers College Press, 1983.

19. Wohl, Agnes and Kaufman, Bobbie: *Silent Screams and Hidden Cries (An Interpretation of Artwork by Children from Violent Homes).* New York, Brunner/Mazel, 1985.

Individual Therapy with Children

1. Bornstein, Philip and Kazdin, Alan E. (Eds.): *Handbook of Clinical Behavior Therapy With Children.* Homewood, Dorsey Press, 1985.

2. Caret, Donald: *Principles of Child Psychotherapy.* Springfield, Charles C Thomas, 1972.

3. Cooper, S. and Wasserman, L.: *Children in Treatment: A Primer for Beginning Psychotherapists.* New York, Brunner/Mazel, 1985.

4. Daws, Dilys and Boston, Mary: *The Child Psychotherapist.* London, Wildwood House, 1977.

5. Graziano, Anthony: *Behavior Therapy with Children,* Vol. 1. Chicago, Aldine, 1971.
6. Graziano, Anthony: *Behavior Therapy with Children,* Vol. 2. Chicago, Aldine, 1975.
7. Kagan, R. M.: Storytelling and game therapy for children in placement. *Child Care Quarterly, 11*(4), 280-290, 1982.
8. Kashani, Javad H.: Current perspectives on childhood depression: an overview. *American Journal of Psychiatry, 138*(2), 143-153, 1981.
9. Keat, Donald: *Fundamentals of Child Counseling.* Boston, Houghton Mifflin, 1974.
10. Lieberman, Florence: *Social Work with Children.* New York, Human Sciences Press, 1979.
11. Lord, Joseph P.: *A Guide to Individual Psychotherapy with School Age Children and Adolescents.* Springfield, Charles C Thomas, 1985.
12. Mishner, Judith: *Clinical Work with Children.* New York, Free Press, 1983.
13. Schaefer, Charles E. (Ed.): *Therapeutic use of Child's Play.* New York, Jason Aronson, 1976.

APPENDIX B

ASSESSMENT SCALES/RATINGS

Child Assessment Scales/Procedures

1. Activity Counseling
   Elementary School Ages, 1972

   McComb, B.: *Activity counseling: an individual counseling procedure for the elementary school child.* Unpublished manuscript, Nova Elementary School, Fort Lauderdale, Fla., 1972.

2. Assessment of Coping Style
   Grades kgn-8, 9-12, 1981
   Herbert F. Boyd and G. Orville Johnson

   Charles E. Merrill Publishing Co.
   1300 Alum Creek Drive
   Columbus, Ohio, 43216

3. Biblio-therapy
   All age groups, 1971

   Moody, Mildred T., Hannigan, Margaret C., Kinney, Margaret M., Kircher, Clara, J. and Limper, Hilda K.: *Biblio-Therapy.* Chicago, American Library Association, 1971.

4. Blackboard Drawings
   Elementary Age Children, 1970

   Mackay, D.: *Treatment for Children.* New York, Science House, 1970.

5. Bloom Sentence Completion Survey
   Ages 6-21, adults, 1974-75
   Wallace Bloom

   Stoelting Company
   1350 S. Kostner Avenue
   Chicago, IL 60623

6. Cain-Levine Social Competency Scale
   Mentally Retarded Children ages 5-13, 1963
   Leo F. Cain, Samuel Levine and Freeman F. Elzey

   Consulting Psychologists Press, Inc.
   577 College Avenue
   Palo Alto, CA 94306

7. California Test of Personality
Grades kgn-3, 4-8, 7-10, 9-14, adults, 1939-1953
Louis P. Thorpe, Willis W. Clark and Ernest W. Tiegs

CTB/McGraw-Hill Book Co., Inc.
1221 Avenue of the Americas
New York, NY 10020

8. Child and Adolescent Adjustment Profile
Children and adolescents, 1977-81
Robert B. Ellsworth and Shanae L. Ellsworth

Consulting Psychologists Press, Inc.
577 College Avenue
Palo Alto, CA 94306

9. Child Anxiety Scale
Grades kgn-5, 1980
John S. Gillis

Institute for Personality and Ability Testing, Inc.
Test Services Division
P.O. Box 188
Champaign, IL 61820

10. Child Depression Inventory
Ages 7-17 years, 1977

Kovacs, M. and Beck, A. T.: An empirical-clinical approach toward a definition of childhood depression. In Schulterbrandt, Joy G. and Taskin, Allen (Eds.): *Depression in Childhood: Diagnosis, Treatment, and Conceptual Models.* New York, Raven Press, 1977, pp. 1-25.

11. Children's Apperception Test
Ages 3-10, 1949-1974
Leopold Bellak, Sonya Sorel Bellak, Mary R. Haworth (checklist) and Marvin S. Huervich (manual)

C.P.S., Inc.
P.O. Box 83
Larchmont, NY 10538

12. Children's Depression Scale
Ages 9-16, 1978
Moshe Lang and Miriam Tistea

Australian Council for Educational Research
P.O. Box 210
Hawthorn, Victoria, Australia 3122

13. Children's Embedded Figures Test
Ages 5-12, 1963-1971
Stephen A. Karp, Norma Konstadt (test) and manual coauthors, Herman A. Witkin, Philip K. Oltman and Evelyn Raskin.

Consulting Psychologists Press, Inc.
577 College Avenue
Palo Alto, CA 94306

14. Children's Inventory of Anger
Children with at least a fourth grade reading level, 1978

Nelson, W. M., III and Finch, A. J. Unpublished manuscript, Xavier University

260

15. Children of Alcoholics Screening Test
    Children of alcoholics, 1981-1982
    John W. Jones

    Camelot Press
    Attention: Dr. John W. Jones
    1812 Rolling Green Curve
    Mendola Heights, MN 55118

16. Children's Manifest Anxiety Scale
    Children, 1956

    Castaneda, Alfred; McCandless, Boyd R.; and Palmero, David: The children's form
    of manifest anxiety scale. *Child Development, 27,* 217-326, 1956.

17. Coopersmith Self-Esteem Inventories
    Ages 8-15, 16 and above, 1981
    Stanley Coopersmith

    Consulting Psychologists Press, Inc.
    577 College Avenue
    Palo Alto, CA 94306

18. Culture-Free Self-Esteem Inventories for Children and Adults
    Grades 3-9 and adults, 1981
    James Battle

    Special Child Publications
    4535 Union Bay Place, N.E.
    Seattle, WA 98105

19. Early School Personality Questionnaire
    Ages 6-8, 1966-76
    Richard W. Coan and Raymond B. Cattell

    Institute for Personality and Ability Testing, Inc.
    Test Services Division
    P.O. Box 188
    Champaign, IL 61820

20. Education Apperception Test
    Preschool and Elementary School, 1973
    Jack M. Thompson and Robert A. Jones

    Western Psychological Services
    12031 Wilshire Blvd.
    Los Angeles, CA 90025

21. Family Relations Test
    Ages 3-7, 7-15, adults, 1957-1978
    Eva Bene and James Anthony

    NFER-Nelson Publishing Co.
    Darville House
    2 Oxford Road East
    Windsor Berkshire
    SL4 1DF, England

22. Fear Survey for Children
    Children, 1964

    Wolpe, J. and Lang, P. A fear survey schedule for use in behavior therapy. *Behavior
    Research and Therapy, 2,* 27-30, 1964.

23. Foren Structured Sentence Completion
    Ages 10-18, adults, 1957-1967
    Bertram R. Foren

    Western Psychological Services
    12031 Wilshire Blvd.
    Los Angeles, CA 90025

24. Goodenough-Harris Drawing Test
    Ages 3-15, 1926-1963
    Florence L. Goodenough and Dale B. Harris

    The Psychological Corporation
    757 Third Avenue
    New York, NY 10017

25. Hassles Scale
    Children and adolescents, 1981

    Kanner, Allen D., Coyne, James C., Schafer, Catherine and Lazarus, Richard S.
    Comparison of two modes of stress management: daily hassles and uplifts versus
    major life events. *Journal of Behavioral Medicine, 4,* 1-39, 1981

26. House, Tree, Person Test
    Children, 1950
    J. N. Buck

    Western Psychological Services
    12031 Wilshire Blvd.
    Los Angeles, CA 90025

27. The Jesness Inventory
    Disturbed Children and Adolescents ages 8-18, adults, 1962-1972
    Carl F. Jesness

    Consulting Psychologists Press, Inc.
    577 College Avenue
    Palo Alto, CA 94306

28. Life Events Scales for Children and Adolescents
    Ages 6-11, 12 and over, 1981
    R. Beam Coddington

    Stress Research Co.
    48 Neron Place
    New Orleans, LA 70118

29. Louisville Fear Survey
    Ages 6-12, 1967

    Miller, Louick, C.: Louisville behavior checklist for males 6-12 years of age. *Psychological Reports, 21,* 885-896, 1967.

30. Machover Draw-a-Person Test
    Ages 2 and over, 1949
    Karen Machover

    Charles C Thomas, Publisher
    2600 South First Street
    Springfield, IL 62794-9265

31. Make-a-Family Test

    Malecki, D.: *Make-a-family test.* Unpublished test. Pennsylvania State University, 1972.

32. Make a Picture Story
    Ages 6 and over, 1947-1952
    Edwin S. Shneidman

    The Psychological Corporation
    757 Third Avenue
    New York, NY 10017

33. Make a Story Procedure—use pictures from:

    Mead, M. and Heyman, K. *Family.* New York, Macmillan, 1965.

34. Matching Familiar Figures Test
    Ages 5-12, 13 and over, 1965
    Jerome Kagan (test) and Neil J. Salkind (norms booklet)

    Jerome Kagan
    Harvard University
    Kirkland Street
    1510 William James Hall
    Cambridge, MA 02138

35. Maxfield-Buchholz Scale of Social Maturity for Use with Preschool Blind Children
    Infancy-6, 1958
    Kathryn E. Maxfield and Sandra Buchholz

    American Foundation for the Blind, Inc.
    15 West 16th Street
    New York, NY 10011

36. The Michigan Picture Test—Revised
    Ages 8-14, 1953-1980
    Max L. Hutt

    Grune & Stratton, Inc.
    111 Fifth Avenue
    New York, NY 10003

37. Missouri Children's Picture Series
    Ages 5-16, 1971
    Jacob O. Sines, Jerome D. Parker and Lloyd K. Sines

    Psychological Assessment and Services, Inc.
    P.O. Box 1031
    Iowa City, IA 52244

38. Mutual Storytelling
    Elementary School ages, 1971

    Gardner, Richard: *Therapeutic Communication with Children.* New York, Science House, 1971

39. Personality Inventory for Children
    Ages 3-16, 1977
    Robert D. Wirt, Philip D. Seat, David Lochaa (manual), James K. Klinedinst (manual) and William E. Broen (test)

Western Psychological Services
12031 Wilshire Blvd.
Los Angeles, CA 90025

40. Personality Rating Scale or Child Personality Scale
    Grades 4-12, 1944-1962
    S. Mary Amatora

    Educators'-Employers' Tests and Services Associates
    120 Detzel Place
    Cincinnati, OH 45219

41. The Picture World Test
    Ages 6 and over, 1955-1965
    Charlotte Buhler and Morse P. Manson

    Western Psychological Services
    12031 Wilshire Blvd.
    Los Angeles, CA 90025

42. The Piers-Harris Children's Self-Concept Scale (The Way I Feel About Myself)
    Grades 3-12, 1969
    Ellen V. Piers and Dale B. Harris

    Counselor Recordings and Test
    P.O. Box 6184, Ackler Station
    Nashville, TN 37212

43. Primary Self-Concept Inventory
    Grades kgn-6, 1973-1974
    Douglas G. Muller and Robert Leonetti

    Teaching Resources Corporation
    50 Pond Rack Road
    Hingham, MA 02043

44. The Q-Toys Tests of Personality
    Ages 6 and over, 12 and over, 1967-1969
    Arthur G. Storey and Louis I. Masson

    Institute of Psychological Research, Inc.
    34 Ovest, Rue Fleury Streetwest
    Montreal, Quebec, Canada

45. The Quality of School Life Questionnaire
    Grades 4-12, 1977-1978
    Joyce L. Epstein under the direction of James M. McPartland, Johns Hopkins University

    Riverside Publishing Company
    8420 Bryn Mawr Avenue
    Chicago, IL 60631

46. A Reinforcement Survey Schedule for Children, in:

    Keat, Donald B.: *Fundamentals of Child Counseling.* Boston, Houghton Mifflin, 1974

47. Relaxation Exercises
    All ages, 1972

Keat, Donald B.: Broad-spectrum behavior therapy with children: a case presentation. *Behavior Therapy, 3,* 454-459, 1972.

48. School-Attitude Measure
Grades 4-6, 7-8, 9-12, 1980
Lawrence J. Dolen and Marci Morrow Enos

American Testronics
209 Holiday Road
Coralville, IA 52241

49. School Attitude Survey: Feelings I Have About School
Grades 3-6, 1970
Harold F. Burks

Arden Press
8331 Alvaredo Drive
Huntington Beach, CA 92646

50. The Self-Concept and Motivation Inventory: What Face Would You Wear?
Ages 4-kgn, grades 1-3, 3-6, 7-12, 1967-1977.
George A. Farrah, Norman J. Milehus and William Reitz

Person-o-Metrics, Inc.
20504 Williamsburg Road
Dearborn Heights, MI 48127

51. Self-Concept Adjective Checklist
Grades kgn-8, 1971
Alan J. Politte

Psychologists and Educators, Inc.
Sales Division
211 West State Street
Jacksonville, IL 62650

52. Self-Concept as a Learner Scale
Grades 4-12, 1967-1972
Walter B. Waetjen

Author at Cleveland State University
Cleveland, OH 44115

53. Self-Esteem Questionnaire
Ages 9 and over, 1971-1976
James K. Hoffmeister

Test Analysis and Development Corporation
2400 Park Lane Drive
Boulder, CO 80301

54. Self-Observation Scale
Grades kgn-6, 1974
A. Jackson Stenner and William G. Katzenmeyer

NTS Research Corporation
Durham, NC

55. Self-Perception Inventory
Grades 1-12, high school age and adult, 1965-1980
Anthony T. Soares and Louise M. Soares

SOARES Associates
111 Teeter Rock Road
Trumbull, CT 06611

56. Squiggle Game Procedure
All ages, 1971

Winnicott, Donald W.: *Therapeutic Consultations in Child Psychiatry.* New York, Basic Books, 1971.

57. Social Readjustment Rating Scale for Children
Children and older, 1967

Holmes, Thomas H. and Rahe, Richard H.: The social readjustment scale. *Journal of Psychosomatic Research, 11,* 213-218, 1967.

58. STATE-Trait Anxiety Inventory for Children
Ages 4-6, 1970-1973
Charles D. Spielberger in collaboration with C. Drew Edwards, Robert E. Lushene, Joseph Montuori and Danna Platzen

Consulting Psychologists Press, Inc.
577 College Avenue
Palo Alto, CA 94306

59. The Stick-Man Procedure

Leman, L. *The stick-man procedure.* Unpublished test, Pennsylvania State University, 1972.

60. Suppertime Drawings

Leubischer, F. *Family supper-time drawing procedure.* Unpublished manuscript, Pennsylvania State University, 1972.

61. Tasks of Emotional Development Test
Ages 6-11, 12-18, 1960-1971
Haskel Cohen and Geraldine Richard Weil

T. E. D. Associates
42 Lowell Road
Brookline, MA 02146

62. Thematic Apperception Test
Ages 4 and over, 1935-1943
Henry A. Murray

Harvard University Press
79 Garden Street
Cambridge, MA 02138

63. Values Inventory for Children
Grades 1-7, 1976
Joan S. Guilford, Willa Gupta and Lisbeth Goldberg

Sheridan Psychological Services, Inc.
P.O. Box 6101
Orange, CA 92667

64. What I Like to Do: An Inventory of Student Interests
Grades 4-7, 1954-1975
C. E. Meyers and manual coauthors, Marcella R. Bonsall, Karen Drinkard, Mary Ellen Nogrady, Linda Metz Organ and Elayne Goldman Zinner.

Science Research Associates, Inc.
155 North Wacker Drive
Chicago, IL 60606

65. What I Think and Feel
Grades 1-12, 1978
Cecil R. Reynolds and Bert Richmond

Cecil R. Reynolds
Dept. of Educational Psychology
University of Georgia
Athens, GA 60602

66. Welsh Figure Preference Test
Ages 6 and over, 1959-1980
George S. Welsh

Consulting Psychologists Press, Inc.
577 College Avenue
Palo Alto, CA 94306

67. Youth Self-Report
Ages 11-18, 1983

Acherbach, Thomas, M. and Edelbrock, Craig.: *Manual for the Child Behavior Checklist and Revised Child Behavior Profile.* Burlington, UT, University Associates in Psychiatry, 1983.

Assessment Ratings/Checklists

1. Adaptive Behavior Scale
Mentally retarded and emotionally disturbed, ages 3-adult, grades 2-6, 1969-1975
Kazuo Nihira, Ray Foster, Max Shellhaas and Henry Leland

American Association on Mental Deficiency
5101 Wisconsin Avenue, N.W.
Washington, D.C. 20016

2. Barclay Classroom Assessment System
Grades 3-6, 1971-1981
James R. Barclay

Western Psychological Services
12031 Wilshire Blvd.
Los Angeles, CA 90025

3. Behavioral Characteristics Progression
Mentally and behaviorally exceptional children, 1973
The Santa Cruz Special Education Management System

VORT Corporation
P.O. Box 11132
Palo Alto, CA 96306

4. Behavior Problem Checklist
1979
Herbert C. Quay, Ph.D. and Donald R. Peterson, Ph.D.

Dr. Herbert C. Quay
P.O. Box 248074
University of Miami
Coral Gables, FL 33124

5. Behavior Problem Checklist—Revised Form
1983
Herbert C. Quay, Ph.D. and Donald R. Peterson, Ph.D.

Dr. Herbert C. Quay
P.O. Box 248074
University of Miami
Coral Gables, FL 33124

6. Burks Behavior Rating Scales
Preschool and kgn, grades 1-8, 1968-1969
Harold F. Burks

Arden Press
8331 Alvarado Drive
Huntington Beach, CA 92646

7. CAAP Scale
Children and adolescents, 1977-1978
Robert B. Ellsworth and Shanae L. Ellsworth

Consulting Psychologists Press, Inc.
577 College Avenue
Palo Alto, CA 94306

8. The California Child Q Sort
Children, 1980
Jeanne Block and Jack Block

Consulting Psychologists Press, Inc.
577 College Avenue
Palo Alto, CA 94306

9. Checklist by Ullman, Sleator and Sprague
Children, 1984

Ullmann, R. K., Sleater, E. K., and Sprague, R. L.: A new rating scale for diagnosis and monitoring for ADD children. *Psychopharmacology Bulletin, 20,* 160-164, 1984.

10. Child Behavior Checklist
Ages 4-18, 1980-1983
Thomas M. Achenbach and Craig Edelbrock

Thomas M. Achenbach
Department of Psychiatry
University of Vermont
Burlington, VT 05401

11. Child Behavior Profile: I
Boys Ages 6-11, 1978

Achenbach, Thomas, M.: The child behavior profile: I. Boys aged 6-11. *Journal of Consulting and Clinical Psychology, 46*(3), 478-488, 1978.

12. Child Behavior Profile: II
Boys 12-16, girls 6-11, and 12-16

Achenbach, Thomas, M.: The child behavior profile: II. Boys aged 12-16 and girls aged 6-11 and 12-16. *Journal of Consulting and Clinical Psychology, 47*(2), 223-233, 1978

13. The Child Behavior Rating Scale
    Grades kgn-3, 1960-1962
    Russell N. Cassel

    Western Psychological Services
    12031 Wilshire Blvd.
    Los Angeles, CA 90025

14. Conners Teacher Rating Scale
    Children, 1969

    Connors, C. Keith: A teacher rating scale for use in drug studies with children. *American Journal of Psychiatry, 126,* 884-888, 1969.

15. Conners Teacher/Parent Rating Scale, Revised Form, 1978

    Goyett, Charles H., Conners, C. Keith and Ulrich, Richard F.: Normative data on Revised Connors Parent and Teacher Rating Scales. *Journal of Abnormal Child Psychology, 6,* 221-236, 1978

16. Daily Behavior System
    Children and adults with behavior problems, 1971-1974
    Jerome J. Stumphauzer

    Behaviormetrics Publishing Co.
    P.O. Box 1168
    Venice, CA 90291

17. Developmental Profile II
    Birth to 9, 1972-1980
    Gerald D. Alpern, Thomas J. Boll and Marsha S. Shearer

    Psychological Developmental Publications
    P.O. Box 3198
    Aspen, CO 81612

18. Devereux Child Behavior Rating Scale
    Emotionally disturbed and mentally retarded children ages 8-12, 1966
    George Spivack and Jules Spotts

    Devereux Foundation Press
    P.O. Box 400
    19 S. Waterloo Road
    Devon, PA 19333

19. Devereux Elementary School Behavior Rating Scale
    Grades kgn-6, 1966-1967
    George Spivack and Marshall Swift

    Devereux Foundation Press
    P.O. Box 400
    19 S. Waterloo Road
    Devon, PA 19333

20. Eyberg Child Behavior Inventory
    Ages 2-16, 1978-1980
    Sheila M. Eyberg

Sheila M. Eyberg
The Oregon Health Sciences University
School of Medicine
Department of Medical Psychology
3181 S.W. Sam Jackson Park Road
Portland, OR 97201

21. The Facial Interpersonal Perception Inventory
Ages 5 and over
Joseph J. Luciani and Richard E. Carney

   Carney, Weedman and Associates
   3308 Military Drive, Suite 835
   San Diego, CA 92110

22. Family Environment Scale
Family members, 1974-1981
Rudolf H. Moos, Bernice S. Moos (manual)

   Consulting Psychologists Press, Inc.
   577 College Avenue
   Palo Alto, CA 94306

23. Inferred Self-Concept
Grades 1-6, 1969-1973
E. L. McDaniel

   Western Psychological Services
   12031 Wilshire Blvd.
   Los Angeles, CA 90025

24. Jesness Behavior Checklist
Ages 10 and over, 1970-1971
Carl F. Jesness

   Consulting Psychologists Press, Inc.
   577 College Avenue
   Palo Alto, CA 94306

25. Louisville Behavior Checklist
Ages 4-7, 7-12, 13-17, 1977-1981
Lovick C. Miller

   Western Psychological Services
   12031 Wilshire Blvd.
   Los Angeles, CA 90025

26. Multi-Dimensional Children's Observation Scale
Ages 5-12, 1980
Susan T. Dennison

   Susan T. Dennison
   5965 S.W. 100th Street
   Miami, FL 33156

27. Observer Rating Scale of Anxiety
Children facing surgery, 1975

   Melamed, Barbara and Siegal, Lawrence: Reduction of anxiety in children facing
   hospitalization and surgery by use of filmed modeling. *Journal of Consulting and
   Clinical Psychology, 43,* 511-521, 1975.

270

28. Ottawa School Behavior Checklist
Ages 6-12, 1967-1969
June B. Pimm and Gordon McClure
Pimm Consultants Ltd.

29. Peer Nomination Inventory for Depression

Lekfowitz, Monroe M. and Tesiny, Edward P.: Assessment of childhood depression. *Journal of Consulting and Clinical Psychology, 48,* 43-50.

30. Personality Inventory for Children
Children, 1977, 1981
Wiet, Robert D., Ph.D., Seat, Philip D., Ph.D., Broen, William E., Ph.D. and Lacher, David, Ph.D.

Western Psychological Services
12031 Wilshire Blvd.
Los Angeles, CA 90025

31. Preschool Behavior Questionnaire
Ages 3-6, 1974
Lenore Behar and Samuel Stringfield

Lenore Behar
State of North Carolina
Dept. of Human Resources
Albemorale Building
325 N. Salisbury Street
Raleigh, NC 27611

32. Rating of Behavior Scale
Children, Adolescents and Adults, 1980
Richard E. Carney

Carney, Weedman and Associates
3308 Military Drive, Suite 835
San Diego, CA 92110

33. Rating Scale by Pelham and Bender
Hyperactive children, 1981

Peer relationships in hyperactive children: description and treatment. In Gadow, Kenneth D. and Bialer, Irv (Eds.): *Advances in Learning and Behavioral Disabilities,* Vol. 1. Greenwich, CN, Jai Pr, 1981, pp. 365-436.

34. Rimland's Diagnostic Checklist for Disturbed Children Differentiates children with Kawner's syndrome or early infantile autism from children with other developmental disabilities.

Rimland, Bernard: *Infantile Autism.* New York, Appleton-Century-Crofts, 1964.

35. Scales of Independent Behavior
Children, 1984
Robert H. Brenninks, Richard W. Woodcock, Richard F. Weatherman and Bradley K. Hill

DLM Teaching Resources
One DLM Park
Allen, TX 75002

36. Self-Administered Dependency Questionnaire
Ages 8-15, 1973-1974
Ian Berg

Ian Berg
Highlands Adolescent Unit
Scalebor Park, Burley-in-Whanfedale
Ilkley, Yorkshire, LS29 7AY, England

37. Self-Concept Adjective Checklist
Grades kgn-8, 1971
Alan J. Politte

Psychologists and Educators, Inc.
Sales Division
211 West State Street
Jacksonville, IL 62650

38. Scales for Rating the Behavioral Characteristics of Superior Students
Grades 4-6, 1976
Joseph S. Renzulli, Linda H. Smith, Alan J. White, Carolyn M. Callahan and Robert
K. Hartman.

Creative Learning Press, Inc.
P.O. Box 320
Mansfield Center, CT 06250

39. School Behavior Checklist
Ages 4-6, 7-13, 1977-1981
Louick C. Miller

Western Psychological Services
12031 Wilshire Blvd.
Los Angeles, CA 90025

40. School/Home Observation and Referral System
Preschool-grade 3, 1978
Joyce Evans

CTB/McGraw-Hill
Del Monte Research Park
Monterey, CA 93940

41. Social Behavior Assessment
Grades kgn-6, 1978-1980
Thomas M. Stephens

Cedars Press, Inc.
P.O. Box 29351
Columbus, OH 43229

42. Vineland Social Maturity Scale
Birth to maturity, 1935-1965
Edgar A. Doll

American Guidance Service
Publishers' Building
Circle Pines, MN 55014

43. Walker Problem Behavior Identification Checklist
Grades 4-6, 1970
Hill M. Walker

Western Psychological Services
12031 Wilshire Blvd.
Los Angeles, CA 90025

44. Werry, Weiss, and Peters Activity Scale
Hyperactive children, 1970

Werry, J. and Sprague, R.: Hyperactivity. In C. G. Costello (Ed.): *Symptoms of Psychopathology.* New York, Wiley, 1970, pp. 397-417.

Assessment Interview Schedules

1. Bellevue Index of Depression (1978)

Petti, Theodore, A.: Depression in hospitalized child psychiatry patients. Approaches to measuring depression. *American Academy of Child Psychiatry, 17,* 49-59, 1978.

2. Children's Depression Rating Scale

Pozanski, E. O., Cook, S. C. and Carroll, B. J.: A depression rating scale for children. *Pediatrics, 64,* 442-450, 1979.

3. Interview Schedule for Children

Kovacs, M.: Interview schedule for children. University of Pittsburgh School of Medicine, Pittsburgh, PA

4. Kiddie-SADS
6-16 years of age
Chambers, W. J. and Puig-Antich, J. In:

Kazdin, Ian E.: Assessment techniques for childhood depression. *American Academy of Child Psychiatry, 20,* 358-375, 1981.

5. Precipitant Interview for Asthmatic Patients

Percell, L. and Weiss, J. H.: Asthma. In Costello, Charles G. (Ed.): *Symptoms of Psychopathology: A Handbook.* New York, John Wiley and Sons, Inc., 1970, pp. 597-623.

6. Whalen and Henker Structured Interviews

Whalen, Carol K. and Henker, Barbara (Eds.): *Hyperactive Children: The Social Ecology of Identification and Treatment.* New York, Academic Press, 1980.

APPENDIX C

ADDITIONAL ACTIVITIES FOR
INDIVIDUAL THERAPY

1. Anderson, Fay Bennett: *Fay's First Fifty: Activities for the Young and Severely Handicapped.* August, Fact, 1974.
2. Arnold, Arnold: *The World Book of Children's Games.* Greenwich, Fawcett Publications, 1972.
3. Barry, Sheila Anne: *Super-Colossal Book of Puzzles, Tricks, and Games.* New York, Sterling Publishing Company, 1978.
4. Berenstain, Stan and Berenstain, Jan: *The Bears' Activity Book.* New York, Random House, 1979.
5. Braga, Joseph and Braga, Laurie: *Children and Adults—Activities for Growing Together.* Englewood Cliffs, Prentice-Hall, 1976.
6. Caney, Steven: *Kids America.* New York, Workman Publishers, 1978.
7. D'Amato, Janet and D'Amato, Alex: *U.S.A. Fun and Play.* Garden City, Doubleday and Company, 1966.
8. Davis, Duane: *My Friends and Me.* Circle Pines, American Guidance Services, 1977.
9. Dinkmeyer, Don: *Developing Understanding of Self and Others.* Circle Pines, American Guidance Service, 1970.
10. Dupont, Henry; Gardner, Sue Ovitta; and Brody, David S.: *Toward Affective Development.* Circle Pines, American Guidance Service, 1974.
11. Hendricks, Gary and Wills, Russel: *The Centering Book.* Englewood Cliffs, Prentice-Hall, 1975.
12. Kline, Judy: *Children Move to Learn: A Guide to Planning Gross Motor Activities.* Columbus, Ohio State University, Tucson, Communication Skill Builders, 1977.
13. Krughoff, G. G. et al.: *Super Me—Super You: A Bilingual Activity Book for Young Children.* Washington, D.C.; U.S. Dept. of Health, Education, and Welfare, 1979.
14. Kaplan, Phyllis; Kohfeldt, Joyce; and Sturra, Kim. *It's Positively Fun.* Denver, Love Publishing Company, 1974.
15. Margaret, Mary: *Media Magic.* Washington, D.C., Aeropolis Books, 1979.
16. Marzollo, Jean and Lloyd, Janice: *Learning Through Play.* New York, Harper and Row, Publishers, 1972.

APPENDIX D

CHILDREN'S BOOKS AND MAGAZINES

Books

1. Alexander, Martha: *Nobody Asked Me If I Wanted a Baby Sister.* New York, The Dial Press, 1971.
2. Armstrong, Louise: *How to Turn War Into Peace.* New York, Harcourt, Brace, Jovanovich, 1979.
3. Arnstein, Helene S.: *Billy and Our New Baby.* New York, Human Sciences Press, 1973.
4. Barrett, John M.: *Daniel Discovers Daniel.* New York, Human Sciences Press, 1979.
5. Barrett, John M.: *No Time for Me.* New York, Human Sciences Press, 1978.
6. Barrett, John M.: *Oscar the Selfish Octopus.* New York, Human Sciences Press, 1978.
7. Berger, Terry: *I Have Feelings.* New York, Behavioral Publications, 1971.
8. Berger, Terry: *I Have Feelings, Too.* New York, Behavioral Publications, 1979.
9. Bergstrom, Corinne: *Losing Your Best Friend.* New York, Human Sciences Press, 1980.
10. Blue, Rose: *Wishful Lying.* New York, Human Sciences Press, 1980.
11. Cohen, Miriam: *Will I Have a Friend?* New York, Collier Books, 1967.
12. Fassier, Joan: *All Alone with Daddy.* New York, Behavioral Publications, 1969.
13. Fassier, Joan: *Boy with a Problem.* New York, Behavioral Publications, 1971.
14. Fassier, Joan: *My Grandpa Died Today.* New York, Behavioral Publications, 1971.
15. Fassier, Joan: *The Man of the House.* New York, Behavioral Publications, 1969.
16. Gardner, R.: *Dr. Gardner's Stories about the Real World.* Englewood Cliffs, Prentice-Hall, 1973.
17. Green, Phyllis: *A New Mother for Martha.* New York, Human Sciences Press, 1978.
18. Guilfoile, Elizabeth: *Nobody Listens to Andrew.* New York, Scholastic Book Sciences, 1957.
19. Hazen, Barbara Shook: *Two Homes to Live In.* New York, Human Sciences Press, 1977.
20. Heide, Florence Parry: *Some Things are Scary.* New York, Scholastic Book Services, 1969.
21. Kraus, Robert: *Leo the Late Bloomer.* New York, Windmill Books and E.P. Dutton, 1971.

22. Sinbergstenson, Janet: *Now I Have a Stepparent and It's Kind of Confusing.* New York, Avon Books, 1979.

23. Viorst, Judith: *Alexander and the Terrible, Horrible, No Good, Very Bad Day.* Connecticut, Atheneum, 1972.

24. Viorst, Judith: *The Tenth Good Thing About Barney.* Connecticut, Atheneum, 1971.

Magazines

1. *Child Life Magazine,* Saturday Evening Post Co., Youth Publications, 1100 Waterway Boulevard, P.O. Box 567B, Indianapolis, Indiana 46206.
2. *Children's Playmate,* 1100 Waterway Boulevard, P.O. Box 567B, Indianapolis, Indiana, 46206.
3. *Cricket Magazine,* P.O. Box 100, LaSalle, Illinois 61301.
4. *Ebony, Jr.,* Johnson Publishing Co., 820 S. Michigan Avenue, Chicago, Illinois 60605.
5. *Electric Company Magazine,* P.O. Box C-19, Birmingham, Alabama 35282.
6. *Highlights for Children,* 803 Church Street, Honesdale, Pennsylvania 18431.
7. *Humpty Dumpty's Magazine,* Parents Magazine Enterprise, Inc., 52 Vanderbilt Avenue, New York, New York 10017.
8. *Jack and Jill,* 1100 Waterway Boulevard, P.O. Box 567B, Indianapolis, Indiana 46206.
9. *Listen Magazine,* 6830 Laurel Street, N.W., Washington, D.C. 20012.
10. *Ranger Rick's Nature Magazine,* National Wildlife Federation, 1412 16th Street, N.W., Washington, D.C. 20036.
11. *Sesame Street Magazine,* 123 Sesame Street, P.O. Box 2892, Boulder, Colorado 80322.
12. *World Magazine for Children,* National Geographic Society, P.O. Box 2330, Washington, D.C. 20013.

278

APPENDIX E

SAMPLE CHILD ASSESSMENT FOR
INDIVIDUAL THERAPY

Name of Child: <u>Meghan Howard</u>   Date of Birth: <u>3-10-78</u>

Dates of Assessment: <u>January 10 through March 10, 1985</u>

I. *Referral*

Ms. James, Meghan's second grade teacher, referred her for in-dividual therapy. The reason for this recommendation was Meghan's increased withdrawal behavior since she entered the second grade. Ms. James reports that Meghan completes all of her school work quickly and correctly. However, she has no friends at school and seems unhappy most of the time.

Meghan's mother reports the same behavior at home. She feels it is directly related to her and the child's father divorcing last summer. There are no other professionals currently working with this child or family.

Both Ms. James and Ms. Howard feel the benefit of therapy for Meghan would be to get her to verbalize what has caused her withdrawal.

II. *Description of Child and Session Contact*

Meghan has been seen twice a week for the past two months. She is a cute, seven-year-old, blond, blue-eyed child who came into the sessions being very quiet and with little eye contact. Meghan is about average size for her age and seems to be quite particular about her appearance. She has been well dressed and groomed for all sessions. As indicated by her teacher, Meghan appears to be a bright child who is about a year above grade level in reading and has particularly good memory skills. This child always

279

was in contact with reality in the sessions and seems to have no history of hallucinations.

Meghan did not readily open up in the sessions but, now after two months, has significantly improved her eye contact with this therapist. Her affect has improved, in that it does not appear to be depressed continuously and she has started to spontaneously disclose in the last three sessions. This child has shown a definite ability to form a significant relationship with this therapist.

During these two months of assessment sessions, the following scales and activities were administered: drawings of self and family, books on divorce, squiggle game, Piers-Harris Self Concept Scale, board games, activity sheets, and the Child Depression Inventory.

III. *Assessment Results*

The above scales and activities provided the following significant results:

A. Meghan continues to be very angry with her parents over their divorce.

B. She still feels somewhat responsible for their getting divorced. Meghan has very high expectations of herself and feels she was not a good enough child when her parents were married which is why they had to divorce.

C. Meghan is lonely most of the time because she does not feel she can confide in anyone about these feelings. She is very aware of her withdrawal from peers and is wanting to begin interacting with them again.

D. Meghan finds herself preoccupied frequently with her fantasy of having her mom and dad together again.

IV. *Treatment Recommendations*

Based on the above results, observations, and impressions, it is recommended that Meghan be continued in individual therapy. She has progressed already in both her level of disclosure and overall affect. It is felt that this therapeutic relationship will help Meghan to ventilate and work through her feelings surrounding her parents' divorce.

The goals for individual therapy will be as follows:

1. To decrease Meghan's withdrawal behavior as shown by increased eye contact, improved affect, and more spontaneous sharing with this therapist.

2. To help Meghan work through her feelings around her parents' divorce as shown by more disclosure on this subject and more openness to trying other ways of coping.

These treatment goals will be reassessed after three months of individual therapy on a twice-a-week basis.

Therapist: Susan Dennison, ACSW, LCSW

              Clinical Social Worker

Date: March 15, 1985

APPENDIX F

ANSWERS TO ACTIVITIES

Chapter Three: "Activities Related to Relationship Building/Self Disclosure"

Page

35   *Opposites Game:*

right handed/left handed, thin/fat, tall/short, handsome/un-attractive, curly/straight, slow/fast, dark/light, coordinated/clumsy, sick/healthy, developed/undeveloped

37   *Guess Which Sense!:*

Red-2, Sour-4, Loud-2, Quiet-2, Hot-4,5, Salty-4, Soft-4,5, Furry-4,5, Hard-4,5, Gentle-4,5, Cold-4,5, Sharp-1,4,5, Sweet-4, Rough-1,4,5

42   *Pet Word Completion:*

Fish, Cat, Dog and Bird

49   *Talking Time Opposites Game:*

Morning/night, before school/after school, always/never, doing/resting, upset/happy, good behavior/bad behavior, weekends/weekdays, home/school

50   *Birthday Cake Word Search:*

Six times the word "birthday" is on the cake.

52   *"Special Things I Can Do" Matching:*

Reading/book, Arts and crafts/painting, Skiing/skis, Ball games/football, baseball, bat, Playing an instrument/drums, guitar, Swimming/pool, Dancing/shoes, Singing/music

53   *"Special Things I Can Do" Rebus Puzzle:*

Swim, dance, read, draw, ball games, music

55   *Games Word Scramble:*

Ball games, indoor games, running games, drawing, pretend games, bike riding, board games, card games

Chapter Four: "Activities Related to Affective Awareness and Communication"

Chapter Seven: "Activities Related to School"

Chapter Eight: "Activities Related to Termination and Follow-up"